Hungry People

Hungry People

Stories by Tasha Coryell

Split Lip Press

Published by Split Lip Press
333 Sinkler Road
Wyncote, PA 19095
www.splitlippress.com

ISBN: 978-1721553457

Cover Art by Jayme Cawthern

For Zach, who loved good things and trash things unabashedly.

Table of Contents

Will Work 4 Food

The homeless man moved in two weeks after fall semester classes started. At first I assumed my roommate had brought another fraternity brother home to sleep with, but she said no, she had never seen him before in her life. He was awfully dirty and toothless for a fraternity brother and he wasn't wearing the requisite pledge polo shirt and white sneakers. His sneakers might have been white at one time but had since become caked with a greenish layer of mud.

"I do have some standards, you know," she said when I asked.

The homeless man taped a sign that said "will work 4 food" on the wall next to our poster of a shirtless Channing Tatum and my roommate's collage of her best friends from high school. He put his toothbrush which wasn't a toothbrush at all but a stick with some twigs tied to it with a string in my shower caddy. He asked if he could eat one of my packets of ramen noodles and I said that was okay because they only cost fifty cents in the school store.

When I came back from class, the homeless man was watching cartoons and carving a little person out of a rock. I noticed that he had already carved several little people out of rocks and placed them on my roommate's desk. A colony of little rock people.

I sat on the floor and watched cartoons with him. It had been a long time since I'd watched a cartoon and I felt very small and comforted.

I asked the homeless man if he wanted to go down to the cafeteria with me and get some dinner and he said yes. He filled up several trays of food at the buffet. I told him I'd never seen anyone take advantage of the cafeteria like that before and he smiled.

My roommate wanted to get rid of the homeless man. She said that he smelled and blocked access to her bed. She kicked him in the back a couple of times and he grunted and refused to move. He pulled his sleeping bag over his head. His sleeping bag was nice and new, a bright fuchsia color. I didn't know where he got it until a couple weeks later I saw a sign on the bulletin board asking about a stolen sleeping bag.

I came back from a History Club meeting one day to find that the homeless man was writing one of my papers for me.

"I'm really an engineer, you know," he said. He also told me that he was an astronaut, the president, and a pop star. I got a D on the paper, but I told him it was okay, I didn't really need a good grade anyway. He smiled. I made us a bag of popcorn and we watched a movie together.

The homeless man and I were getting a little tired of my roommate who sometimes smoked pot in the room and came home late every night, waking us up.

"I need my beauty sleep," the homeless man said.

One night when she staggered in, her makeup smeared and bits of vomit exiting her nose, and fell, instantly, into a deep and drunk sleep, we carried her dead-weight body out the door, across the campus, and down by the river. We took down her collage of her best friends and her framed picture of her parents. We emptied her drawer of all her shorts and sorority shirts and put them in a box and set them next to where she lay snoring.

I expected her to come back in the morning, furious and spewing at me with her alcohol-breath. When she didn't, I grew worried that she had wandered into the river and died as had the missing fraternity brother the year before, so the homeless man and I got into my car and drove past where we dumped her. We found her sitting on the side of the road, her collage of friends turned to the backside and on it, written in pink marker, was a note that said, "Will work 4 food."

Her dress had ripped at some point in the night. One of her breasts was exposed and somewhere she had found a pack of cigarettes to smoke.

On nights when we have nothing else to do, when there's nothing on TV and none of the clubs I'm involved in have meetings and when the homeless man has run out of rocks to carve into little rock people, we sometimes go stare at my roommate lying there on the side of the road, her blonde hair dirty and tangled.

"She lives like an animal," he says.

"Yes," I agree. "Animal."

Love Like Cheeto Residue That Never Comes Off The Fingers

The nails started popping out of the ceiling like rain. Just pop, pop, pop, all in a row. Some shoddy construction that was, if the nails could come out like that. The floorboard creaked above her, pop, pop, pop.

It was probably a ghost or something. She'd seen that stuff on television, those ghost-hunting shows. The most they ever found were some noises, maybe a glimmer of light or an unexplained movement, but the mundane nature of it made it more real. If they were going to fake it, they could fake it good, like all those shows about rich housewives.

But pop, pop, pop, it just kept raining and she went into her son's room where he was sleeping.

"What's going on, Mama?" She turned the light on and moved his desk chair so she could open the hatch to the attic.

"Just a raccoon or something, go back to sleep."

She walked up the flimsy stairs that descended down from the ceiling and pulled the cord to turn on the light. There was a bundle of something on the floor, but she couldn't quite make out was it was, a bunch of winter coats wrapped around each other. Some animals must've made a nest or something. She went to lift up the coats when they started moving.

"Oh Jesus," she said.

It was a man, the kind that used to be hers. The stench of feces floated past her nose. He didn't smell so different from an animal.

"Adam?"

She stood between him and the stairs, but when he approached her, she backed away. She wasn't yet convinced that he wasn't a poltergeist, some ghost-from-her-past sort of shit.

"George!" she shrieked to her son, "Go into your sister's room!"

His footsteps on the stairs were real, like the sound of pop, pop, pop.

She could hear him running and she went after him, but he was already outside of the house and on the street. He turned back and smiled. He always had been a smiley man.

"Adam, what were you doing in my house?" she yelled. "Adam!" And she thought he might've been an apparition after all, by the way that he disappeared into the night.

She stood on the street not moving because what's a woman to do when the past shows up in the attic like that?

Her daughter came running out of the house, "Mama, what's wrong, what happened?"

"Adam was in the attic," she said and it must've made no sense or something because her daughter asked her, what, say it again, and she had to repeat herself over and over again until they went inside and called 911.

They met when she was twenty and finishing her second year of community college and about to get her associate's degree in business. He was working in a gas station and boy did he gas her up. She went in there to buy some Cheetos and one of those big drinks that only cost seventy-five cents.

"It's free today," he said.

"Why?" she asked.

"Just take it," he said. "Don't you know when somebody tells you to take something, you should just go."

And she took that big bag of Cheetos and ate the whole thing and licked her cheesy fingers and went back the next day to buy another bag.

She got real fat for a little while like that. He gave her donuts too, those glazed ones with the sprinkles on top. They didn't count those, he said. At the end of the day, they just had to throw away whatever was leftover and if he could put it in her sweet mouth instead, that was all right with him.

And she liked how he called her mouth sweet and the way she could feel his eyes on her ass even though he couldn't make manager at that shitty gas station because he skipped too many of his shifts.

"But I'll stop skipping for you, baby," he said.

She let him take her out on their first date a month later. She held out for so long because she wasn't needy like that and she had to do a lot of school work anyway. Those classes the last semester of community college weren't easy and she was working a full time job too, and it was hard to find a night to take off, but she had one Friday free and he had one Friday scheduled, so he picked her up from her studio apartment in a car so beat up that the door didn't lock and she couldn't find the seatbelt and he said, "It's buried somewhere in the seat."

He drove to a fast-food restaurant and parked outside.

"Do you want to go in or get it to go?" he asked.

They got their food to go and had sex in the backseat of the car. There were French fries and ketchup everywhere, and afterwards, as he dipped his squished hamburger into the ketchup lake of her belly button, he said, "Girl, I've been wanting to do that to you since the first day we met."

"I don't know why I let you put your hands on me when I know you're not going anywhere," she said, sipping the rest of her soda.

"Girl, I'll take you places," he said.

"We both know that's not true."

He brought her Cheetos instead of flowers whenever he came to pick her up, his car creaking. When she graduated, he met her parents and while he was in the bathroom of the all-you-can-eat buffet, they said, "Well, you're going to dump him now that you're a college graduate," and she nodded and was embarrassed by all the Jell-O on his plate.

She got a job as a bank teller and he said, "Baby, what are you going to buy me now that you're making all that money?"

"Nothing, baby," she said.

She got her nails done every week because she liked the way that they sounded on the keyboard as she typed in the numbers, click, click, click. The girls who had been there for a long time were faster at it than she was and she studied their technique, click, click, click. Everything about them always felt polished and she invested in some expensive-looking scarves to wrap around her neck and experimented with hairdos that inevitably fell out by the end of the day.

"Woo, baby, you're looking too good for me these days. It's making me worried, I don't know how to keep up with your fancy clothes."

He had been fired from the gas station for not showing up too many times and spent his days on his cousin's couch playing video games. She met his cousin one day when she went to pick him up to go through their favorite drive-thru.

"I want one of those milkshakes," he said. "I like to dip my fries in it."

His cousin sat on the couch with him, wearing a button-up shirt. The cousin was not playing video games, but appeared a momentary spectator wearing shiny shoes. As far as she had seen, none of Adam's clothing had buttons at all. There was a lot of elastic, some zippers. Everything hung loose on him, like a shroud.

"This is my girlfriend," Adam said.

She couldn't remember when she agreed to be his girlfriend. They had never talked about it. He'd said, "Love you, babe," and she'd said, "I need something to eat."

"Nice to meet you," Adam's cousin said.

She knew he was wondering what sort of woman would let this man's penis inside of her, feel the warmth of his gas-station hot-dog sperm. Fast-food French-fry kiss. He was not wrong to wonder this and she could not judge him for it.

"Hold on, baby, I just need to finish a level."

She sat on the edge of a La-Z-Boy chair, watching his video game avatar fight other graphically designed creatures and listening to Adam yell as though he were actually killing them.

"I got you," he said. "I beat the shit out of you. Nothing you can do to stop it."

When they went for food, he paid, and she didn't question where he got the money or if he was going to put a condom on, she just let herself feel that, all the fast-food cum and the liquid felt sort of painful, even though it felt good, the way blood feels when you've first cut yourself. She got a urinary tract infection after that night, everything hot and itchy. Her pee like rotten eggs and she called him and asked, what have you done to me.

He gave her a ring after that, not one of those proposal rings, but the sort of ring a person gives when they want a promise based off nothing. When he gave it to her she said, "Boy, I don't want to know what's in that box," and he said, "But your fingers do," and he put that ring on her finger and she trotted around the bank like the married ladies with houses and dogs and babies.

He presented her with matching earrings the next week and she turned those down saying, "I don't have any holes in my head." She did, but he never looked. She started to get suspicious of where these things were coming from when she watched that diamond sparkle, glittering like a real diamond and not the way the ones from drug stores glowed until they turned the finger green. She wasn't the sort of girl that boys gave diamonds to, but the sort of girl who got Cheetos for free.

"Where are you getting those sparkly things?" she asked him.

"Don't worry about it."

When he called from jail she was surprised only in that he called her, but not about where he was calling her from. He was the sort of person who never had the same number, the sort that could never be saved, but this was the first time he had called from behind bars. He wanted to be bailed out and she said no, those smooth ladies at the bank would never do something like this and she hung up the phone, intent on forgetting about him, and went back to work, click, click, click, that shiny ring still on her finger.

She started getting messages in her email, an address she didn't even know he had. Adaminjail5948 said, hey baby, I miss you. Prisoneradam25 said, if only I could see you naked one more time. Dontdropthesoapadam42443 said, oh please, honey, baby, just show me those titties. She didn't respond, not at first. She would start typing, click, click, click. Ask him when he was getting out, what he was in there for, and no, she was not going to show him her titties, but she couldn't even call them titties or boobies. She had to call them breasts, they were her breasts. As soon as she typed it, before she even reached the period, she would delete it, click, click, click and then block his messages.

She didn't delete his messages completely, but let them pile up in her inbox, one after the other. It was Adam, Adam, Adam, all in a row, all dying for the chance to see her boobs. It turned her on in a way she had never been turned on before and she would sit at the computer and touch herself, her hands outside of her underwear but still wet.

She took her phone, the brand new one she had purchased with a two-year contract. It had a camera on the back and she stripped down naked, held the phone away from her body and snapped pictures of her breasts. She held onto them, squeezing them together. The skin was surprisingly soft and she understood why he enjoyed touching her here, in this way. She looked at the pictures, expecting that she somehow would've been transformed into a porn star, skinny and entirely sexual, but there she was, naked, holding her breasts. She took one last one, sticking her fingers between her legs.

She sent it to all of the addresses from which she had received a message from him. It made her feel so warm and good, imagining him touching himself while looking at her, maybe in front of the other prisoners and the guards. She had never been to a jail, she didn't know what it was like inside, but she could only guess. She wondered if he'd had sex with men. She heard that sort of thing happened in prisons, but couldn't imagine him bent over like that.

As soon as she went to work in the morning and before she went to bed at night, she checked her email to see if he had responded, but he never did. At first she told herself that it was just the prison schedule, he hadn't been allowed to use the computer. After all, it wouldn't be incarceration if they were allowed to do whatever they pleased all the time. She considered that he had gotten in trouble for looking at those pictures of her naked body and this idea pleased her, but finally she just had to concede that he was never going to write back.

She got her own office at the bank, was moved into a manager position. She started going to the gym downstairs to which they got a free membership and lost weight. She learned to do a headstand, picking up her entire body with only the strength of her abdominal muscles. She married a man she found lifting weights and he groaned in the bedroom the same way that he groaned in the gym. They had three children together and bought a house. It was white, Cape Cod style.

When she was pregnant she got heavy Cheeto cravings. Cheetos dipped in peanut butter, Cheetos smashed and used as breadcrumbs. Cheetos as biscuits with gravy. Cheetos sucked and licked so clean that they were white. Her husband brought her Cheetos, but not without judgment.

"Are you sure this is what you want to go into our child's body?" he asked. "What if they come out orange?"

When they got divorced after fifteen years of marriage, the only thing she mourned was the flat-screen television that he took with him in the custody agreement.

She was forty when she heard from him again. She was sipping coffee when she got the message. Coffee upset her stomach, but the bank had a constant supply for customers and over the years she had developed a dependence and either had to choose between a headache and stomach irritation. She was sipping coffee from a mug that one of her sons had decorated for her when he was younger, the scribbles he painted so meaningless and yet so uniquely him. People are so good at being relentlessly themselves. Her email dinged to let her know that she had a new message and she typed click, click, click with her shiny, freshly manicured nails. It was from adamoutsoon355535, hey baby, I'm getting out soon. Let's get together. Hot pics. She deleted that message completely, sent it to a place where it could never come back. She barely remembered who this man was and had only a slight recollection of that body that she showed him all those years ago. She had spent months of her life anticipating this message and when it finally came she was unprepared and her stomach growled in protest of the caffeine and a newly risen hunger.

When she returned home she locked the doors of her little white house, would've tucked her children into bed if they were still at the age where she did such things for them. Wished that her big man with his big groans was still around to protect her. She considered purchasing a gun.

It was suspicious when her doorbell rang one day. Stopping by was a thing that nobody did anymore unless they were selling something and she had earned everything that she had; she had nothing to give. She answered that door though. She was responsible for her actions.

"Adam?"

He had gained weight. Prison had given him a paunch that hung over the edge of his pants. He looked down, the way a dog's tail looks down.

"Hey, baby."

She let him come inside. She had some doors that needed fixing and she didn't want to do it herself. She watched as he sanded that wood down, handled it gently in his hands.

"I think we should get back together, baby."

"But honey, we were never together to begin with."

He started to cry and she couldn't really blame him for that. After all, how many tears had she shed staining all of her pillow covers mascara black after he never responded to her messages? This was her deserved vengeance: she was a bank manager, a home owner, a mother, the kind of woman who said she didn't need a man and meant it.

"Don't come here again, Adam."

It was a crumbling motion if she'd ever seen one. He walked slowly down the street, and she figured at the very least he could stay with that cousin of his, the one with the button-down shirt. She didn't know if his cousin still lived in town or was even still alive. The weird sort of disconnect that occurred when thinking about people from the past. But she didn't want to overthink it. Her doors were fixed and she locked them, listening for the reassuring click.

After she found Adam in the attic, she called the police who told them not to touch the crime scene and asked if anyone was hurt and she said no, even though she felt hurt. The police went up into that attic crawlspace where Adam had been living and carried down reeking buckets of what they later explained was human waste. They kept asking her if she had ever let Adam inside, how much communication they'd had while he was in jail.

"He came over once after he got out," she said. "It was months ago. I didn't give him my address. I don't know how he knew where I lived."

They examined the nails on her floor that had rained down, pop, pop, pop, and said that there was a hole in the attic that Adam had used to look down on her. She thought about all the times she had been naked, her body in front of the mirror. She danced when she was alone, danced while she was getting undressed and there was no music on, and he had seen all these things.

"Let me see your titties one more time, baby."

It hadn't mattered about the pictures. He had found her anyway, naked. Found a perch where he could watch her for always. Took shits above her as she lay in bed, touched himself just seeing her naked body. The police estimated he had been up there for about two weeks, wrapped in her down jacket, feathers starting to poke through the seams.

"Be careful to lock your doors at night," they said, though she couldn't articulate how meaningless that motion was to her now, that click, something supposed to be indicative of safety.

In The Version Where We Work Out

1.

In the version where we work out, I am very beautiful. Not the ordinary kind of beautiful that any old girl can be, but something untouchable. You work in an office. I don't know what you do in the office and it doesn't matter. In your office, you have a nice leather chair that the company paid for. Your office has glass walls that nobody can see into. We have sex in your leather chair and on top of your desk. We have sex more than anyone actually ever has sex. We never get tired.

In the version where we work out, I have a job that I never have to go to except to collect my awards at the yearly banquet for all the good work that I've put in. "It was nothing," I say in my speech and it's true. My dress hugs all the appropriate curves on my body. Everyone comes up to you and tells you how handsome you are and how lucky you are to be with me. We go home to our loft with its exposed brick walls and have sex on the bearskin rug in front of the fireplace. I joke that you killed the bear with your own two hands. You never correct me.

Instead of a child, we birth a condo on an island in the Pacific. We call the condo Sarah. Statistically, you say, that is what our daughter would have been named. Together, we survive a tsunami and it only brings us closer. We fuck as the wind and the water splash around our expensive windows.

In the version where we work out, you only threaten to leave a single time. You've fallen in love with a man at the gym, you say. He has big muscles and a tiny penis. I begin to train for fitness model competitions. I spray my body orange and eat a diet exclusively composed of chicken meat and chicken eggs. I come in last in the competition and you tell me that you think I looked better before, but you stay with me because you don't want to lose custody of Sarah. If I had come in first in the fitness competition, I might have left you. There is no version where this happens.

2.

In the version where we never meet, I am fat and have nice skin. You work at a pizza place that I never go to. You have a girlfriend who is skinny and has bad skin. You don't notice her face. You are too distracted by her hip bones and the way her hair splays out when she goes down on you. I have a boyfriend that resembles a goat. He has big ears and shaggy hair and likes ska music. At seventeen, I still think I am saving myself for something and make him put his dick in my ass instead of my vagina.

In the version where we never meet, you attend the local university and I go somewhere small and faraway. I make plans to lose weight and don't and it's okay. People still love me. You stop taking classes after a year and a half and go back to working at the pizza place. The high school girls still think you're cute, at least for a little while. You never considered what you looked like, what you really looked like, until you tried hitting on the blonde girl with long straight hair and she said, "Gross," and patted down her slices of pizza with napkins.

In college, I go to too many parties and smoke too much weed because I'm so excited to be at a place where people offer me drugs and invite me to parties. I have a B average and my sophomore year I realize that I'm never going to be a doctor and become an art major instead. All of my pieces are sculptures that look like vaginas. I am continuously told that my art degree is worthless and I don't listen because they are talking about my soul.

I get pregnant at the end of junior year. I think about having an abortion. I think about having the baby and filming the pregnancy and making it art. In the end, I have a C-section. I name the baby Sarah. I drop out of school and work at a fast food restaurant where I meet an insurance salesman who says he wants to marry me and I can stay home and work on my art. I make so many vaginas that they don't fit inside my house and I have to set up a vagina display in the backyard. You never touch any of them. You become manager of the pizza place. You become fat with bad skin.

3.

In the version where we don't work out, you call me cute and I say, "Good, because I just got my nose done." You wanted to be a professor and instead you work for a nonprofit. You don't know how to make yourself feel good, but you try so hard.

In the version where we don't work out, your fetish is telling me that you never thought you would date someone like me. Coming from someone else, this would be a compliment. The more beautiful I try to make myself, the more you hate me. You don't like fake breasts, you say. You don't like lipstick or eyeliner. You don't even know who I am when I have that stuff on.

I stop washing my face. I get my breast implants taken out and my chest is like two bags hanging off my bones. I pay a man fifteen dollars to break my nose outside of a bar and he says that he'll do it for free. I only eat dirt and berries, like a caveman. I come home from work to discover you in bed with a girl, Sarah. She looks like I did before, back when you hated me, and you say, "I don't know, Sarah and I are just compatible." I don't know what it means to be compatible, I only know that you don't love me.

We stay together because you don't want to have to move. Who would take the couch? I sit on one end and you sit on the other. Sarah sits between us until she leaves you because she hates being caught in the middle. It is my fault that Sarah leaves. She wouldn't have done so if I had been more beautiful or more invisible. I start getting tattoos. A butterfly on my wrist. A peace sign over the ribs. You say you don't date girls with tattoos and I ask what kind of girls you do date and you describe someone who sounds like a baby that's of legal drinking age. Instead of a tattoo sleeve, I get an entire body. Roots that start on my toes and grow up my calves. Tree branches that stretch across my shoulder blades and leaves that color my face. I stand in the corner of our apartment and scream, "Can you see me?"

The Delivery Driver

She tried to take care of her body. Fruits, vegetables, and whole grains. She restrained her regular pasta cravings to once every several weeks. She drank towering bottles of water like it was necessary for her survival.

Amber liked to cook. She lived alone in a one-bedroom apartment with a windowless kitchen that was never quite clean. Things spilled in the space between the cabinet and the floor and she never stooped to pick these things up. Raisins and walnuts and pits of fruit. The skin of an onion. A leaf of arugula.

To afford a one-bedroom apartment by herself had meant the giving up of other luxuries. A person could have a roommate or a commute and afford to indulge themselves in particular ways that Amber no longer could. A gym membership. The occasional massage. A plethora of avocados. Makeup that couldn't be purchased at the grocery store. It was worth it, she said, to have her own space.

She had a framed poster of Audrey Hepburn on the wall. She'd had this poster since college and still had yet to see an Audrey Hepburn movie. She was preempting her own likes, dictating the kind of person she thought she ought to be. The most expensive thing she owned was a couch. Who knew there was such a huge price for sitting?

She ordered delivery as a treat for herself. It had been a long week at work. She knew that it was bad to use food as a reward. Food as reward encouraged obesity and other things with names that sounded worse than a simple synonym for "largeness." Amber could not control the things her body took pleasure in. It took several steps of weakness before she ordered food into her home.

It used to be that pizza and Chinese were the only thing that could be ordered through delivery. Things that could easily fit themselves into boxes. Things best consumed in the privacy of one's house. But now anything could be wrapped up in paper or Styrofoam and dropped off for a small fee. The car as a server. The earth as restaurant.

Amber ordered a burger. There was one day when she was twelve that she decided she wanted to be a vegetarian and she was for that day. So dedicated for those twenty-four hours. When she woke the following morning her mother was making bacon and she said, "Do you want some, Amber?" and Amber said yes, forgetting her prior declarations of self, the same way she always forgot that she had quit biting her nails.

She reveled in the grease of it. In the fat and the mayonnaise that dripped out of the bun. She had to eat it quickly before the whole thing fell apart. She had not noticed the delivery driver that night. He looked like the other delivery drivers, skinny and white, wearing a baseball cap. It made Amber sad when the driver was old, past the age when it was socially acceptable to drive around another person's meal for a living. She wished there were a way to erase the delivery driver in the delivery experience. A hole in the wall her food could come through. She had never wanted to degrade another human being in order to get sustenance for the evening.

Her order of the burger coincided with a period of illness in her life. It started with a migraine and then a feeling of general malaise that spread across her limbs. Her family practitioner suggested that she was feeling the after-effects of a virus. Amber did not know much about medicine except that viruses were illnesses for which there was no apparent treatment. She followed her doctor's orders to get some rest and took a day off work. She wanted to nip it in the bud, she said.

She lay under a blanket on her expensive couch. Every time she lay on the couch, the expense of her purchase spread a little thinner. That first sit at $2000. How could she ever appreciate that butt-feel? Amber put her hand to her forehead and feigned a fever. The body was hot regardless of the germs that lurked inside. She needed soup. A nice baguette. She had none of these things. The challenges of caring for the body when the body lived alone.

She ordered some soup for delivery. How many times did she have to do something before it verged on habitual? The amounts of money she could spend on her self-pity. It was that same delivery driver, maybe. It was so hard to tell faces apart underneath hats. She said hi. She made sure to tip him extra for his trouble. She did not want him to think less of her, this man that had stood at the entrance of her home who saw her in her sick sweats and her sick T-shirt. The driver had seen her in worse shape than any boyfriend or girlfriend ever had.

She was still feeling sick the following day. She read about things on the internet. Chronic fatigue syndrome. Mono. Immune system disorders that couldn't be categorized by a single doctor's visit. Nothing in her fridge looked appetizing. Some weeks-old apples. Half a loaf of bread. Bread wasn't meant to be refrigerated, but she could never eat the loaves fast enough. She had thought about ordering cookbooks for one. Recipes on sustaining the self. How to consume enough before rot started to form. She didn't though. Surplus seemed like such a stupid problem to have.

She ordered tacos for delivery. There was nothing to justify this. She had worked her way through all of the platitudes and had surrendered to hunger. Basic needs can crowd out other logic. The time between ordering and the time between delivery was meant to be relished. Instead, Amber began to fret over the confines of her body and of her wallet. She could've made toast. Sliced some apples. The guilt of the pre-prepared.

She was noticeably distressed when the driver showed up, that same one, as though he had been waiting to come and see her. Instead of asking for money, he embraced her. Amber had not known that she needed more than food from him until he did this.

Amber had not had a boyfriend since she had broken up with her ex eight months prior. It was so strange how his seemingly innocuous traits of shaming and incessant virility had become suddenly violent in retrospect. Perhaps Amber had never entirely understood what it meant to be loved.

The embrace was not sexual. It felt like the stomach after eating a burrito. It felt like gorging oneself until the body developed an aura of sleepiness. "It's okay," he said. They sat down on her couch together. It was the first time a body besides her body had touched that fabric. "You can eat the tacos," he said. And then he gently pushed the tacos into her mouth. "Chew," he said. Then he stroked her hair until she fell asleep. When she woke, "PAID" was written across the receipt though she had never given him any money.

When she was a child, Amber had gone through another period of illness. First with the chicken pox, and then the flu attacked her weakened immune system. She stopped going to preschool and lay on her childhood couch watching *Sesame Street* and eating bowls of canned chicken noodle soup and scratching the wounds on her body in between oatmeal baths. She longed for a day when she would wake up and feel better and she did feel better, eventually, though it wasn't anything like what she remembered better feeling. She considered, perhaps, that everyone felt at least a little bad every day of their life and that was just the state of humanity.

The night after her encounter with the delivery driver, Amber felt better in a way that she never had before. She had returned to the baseline state of self. Nothing hurt. She had no anxieties, no fears of the day. She was ready to go back to work and fill out forms and make phone calls and write emails, the things that she normally found tedious and unbearable. "Are you feeling better?" asked her coworkers.

"Yes," she said. "I've never felt better. I feel completely rejuvenated." Amber could tell that they were envious of her enlightened state. Even the bags underneath her eyes had dissipated, leaving her face a smooth oval.

Like the day after a good night of sleep, Amber expected her good cheer to last for perpetuity. By lunch, she found herself starting to drag again. She poured herself a cup of coffee. It did nothing but make her hands tremble a little. She logged on to the delivery website. She feared that it would be blocked, the way that the company blocked social networks or porn. It was not against the rules to order food. Everyone needed to eat. Amber still felt like she was transgressing on a dangerous border. Soon, she worried, she would be using proxies to access online dating websites like the sad man that sat in the cubicle next to her.

She ordered pasta. She had never considered pasta to be a midday food. Pasta was a nighttime indulgence. The world was in a fad against carbohydrates. To eat pasta at such a time was the equivalent of eating a piece of cake or a bowl of ice cream. Naughty was the only word she could use to describe how she felt as she entered her work address and clicked the order button. She threw her bag lunch in the trash. No one wanted to eat a lettuce wrap anyway. The best way to ruin a sandwich was to take away the bread and wrap it in lettuce, something that was flavorless and mostly composed of water.

She peered through the glass that lined the doorway of their office-suite. She waited for that hat. For those pseudo-formal black pants. For that ball of a stomach that poked out from underneath the fabric of the T-shirt. For a moment, she thought that it was someone else. Some other delivery driver. But no, it was him. He carried himself so professionally into the office. He carried himself like Amber was not going to pull him into the bathroom stall and make him dish noodles into her mouth like they were Lady and the Tramp, which was what she did.

"What's your name?" she murmured, her mouth full. "Just call me delivery driver," he said. She had almost expected that he would have an exotic sort of accent. Something from France or somewhere, but no, he sounded Midwestern as everyone around her. No one stared as he walked out the door. He was a delivery driver. He belonged everywhere, delivering food.

Amber stopped grocery shopping. She stopped making breakfast in the morning, stopped packing her own lunch, stopped counting calories. It was such a relief to stop doing those things that she thought she would have to do forever. Dishes no longer piled up her sink. Delivery required no dishes. Delivery came with its own dish. Amber's preferred dish was the delivery driver's hand. Food tasted better off that skin as though he carried an inherent seasoning on his fingers.

She stopped going out with friends. She had never been socially capable in the way that her friends were socially capable. Always mistakenly saying something offensive, offhand comments about the worthiness of significant others, something about death, or mentions of substances that leaked out of the body. She left every social gathering with a little bit more self-loathing than she had arrived with, which caused insomnia and skin picking. Amber and the delivery driver rarely spoke. Their relationship surpassed words. Their relationship subsisted on the most basic of human desires: to feed and to be fed.

Amber started getting fat. She had not been thin before. The moment that she first noticed her largeness was standing on a dock at summer camp and realizing that her thighs were the same size as the camp counselor's rather than her peers'. Still, she contained a compulsion that kept her body fat down and enabled her body to fit into spaces that would've otherwise been uncomfortable. The delivery driver enabled her to grow past this. He gave her an excuse to go shopping more. "How constrained I was before," she said to herself.

Amber had assumed a particular monogamy in her relationship with the delivery driver. She often envisioned introducing him to her parents. "Hello, mother," she would say. "This is the man who feeds me." And they would all sit around the table while the delivery driver inserted a bread stick into her mouth, dripping with garlic dipping sauce. It was only once she found another receipt, one with the distinctive "PAID," written across the top that she questioned his loyalty to her hunger.

One night, after a feeding, she got in her car. It creaked with her weight. She followed him from her apartment to a house, one big and glamorous. The delivery driver got out with food, food from a different place than where Amber had ordered. Amber splayed her body across one of the bushes that lined the front of the house. This was the purpose of the bushes, to keep anyone from watching the acts that occurred inside. The branches dug into her stomach, her thighs.

The branches were representative of how she felt as she watched the delivery driver spoon soup into a woman's mouth. The woman was as big and glamorous as the house was. She probably didn't even need to receive her food for free. Amber fell on the ground as she rolled off the bush. She had so little control over how she fell.

When she returned home, Amber placed her second order of delivery for the evening. She had never done this before, ordered twice during the same mealtime. It signaled a certain desperation that she had not previously felt. The delivery driver showed up half an hour later, same as he normally did. He fed her the gyro she had ordered, tahini sauce dribbling down her chin. He did not ask why she needed more, where this hunger had come from. When she finished eating, Amber tried to confront him about the other woman. All he would say was, "We were never really together," and then shook his head slowly. It was so insufficient. She wished he had more food to give her. After he left, she threw up in her toilet. All that it meant was that she had eaten too much. She didn't want to grant too much significance to the whims of her body.

Amber went to the grocery store. It felt so foreign after the previous night's encounter. So many people, so many employees asking how she was. She picked up vegetables and set them down again. They were so raw. They resembled what they were: things that grew on trees and underneath the ground. They did not look edible. She did not know how to put those things in her mouth. Amber bought several frozen dinners. Previously, she had never eaten frozen food. It was high in sodium and never looked like the picture on the box. It was all that she could muster. At the last minute, she added a bottle of white wine to the cart. She had not drunk any alcohol since she last went out with her friends. The wine seemed to make up for some lack of quality in the rest of her groceries.

For dinner, Amber heated up a frozen meal, ate it, and then heated up a second frozen meal because her stomach still rumbled. While she was heating up the third, she realized that she was full, but she ate it anyway because it was already hot and she was never really eating for sustenance to begin with. She poured herself a glass of wine. It was a pinot grigio. It tasted like juice. It tasted like a juice that tasted like nothing. She poured herself another glass. She got so drunk that she found herself ordering delivery. If there had been a selection of "delivery man" on the menu that's what she would've clicked.

It wasn't him. "This isn't my order," Amber said to the pudgy black man who stood at her door. He apologized, so profusely. He would go back and get what she wanted, he said. She looked at his fingers as he clutched the bag. She wondered how they would taste. He made no offer to come inside, though. Everything he could offer surrounded him leaving. "I will comp this meal," he told her. Amber gave him the money anyway. Her purse was flush with the cash that she had stopped using since she was getting all her food for free. She ate what she ordered. It made her feel gassy and gross. She lay on the couch and felt the droplets of sweat on the side of her forehead, the wetness that had gathered underneath her breasts. She rubbed her hand against the fabric. A material sort of comfort.

Super Burger Challenge

Alex had always been good at consuming things, but only if consumption also included a level of destruction. The difference between the thing before it entered the bowels and after.

She'd been let go from her job at Hardwick's 24-Hour Convenience Store and broken up with by her girlfriend in the same week. These things were not unrelated. This was something that Alex was rapidly learning about the self: none of the parts of the body were disconnected.

Alex's girlfriend broke up with her because she was a "selfish, manipulative bitch." Alex said, "Many people have hurt me before you to make me this way," and her girlfriend responded, "That doesn't make it okay." Alex was fired from her job at Hardwick's 24-Hour Convenience Store after checking into the psych ward and missing two shifts because she wasn't allowed to call in sick. She checked out of the ward a mere 36 hours later after deciding that she didn't really need to be there and because she was jonesing for a milk shake.

She stumbled upon the burger-eating contest on accident. Once as a small child she had been snacking on a box of graham crackers and had reached for another unopened plastic pack when she realized that mice had gotten to the crackers before she had and pooped all over the bottom of the box and inside of the plastic seals designed for freshness. She had swallowed crackers gnawed on by the pests, crackers that had resided next to little poop pellets. She considered telling her parents, wondering what sort of diseases that mice could inflict on her small child body. Instead, she kept eating. She was hungry. Her desire to eat the crackers outweighed her disgust. To enter a burger-eating contest was sort of like eating mouse-infested graham crackers only with more or less poop depending on the day.

Alex wasn't good at holding onto friends. They slipped through her fingers like sushi clenched between chopsticks. She got into arguments that she didn't mean, tiny fits that eroded away at any endearment that was left. It was okay, she got new friends that were seemingly better than the old friends until they weren't. Alex met her new friends at the bar down the street from her apartment after she got released from the hospital. She was good at charming people with the woes of her past, good at an intimacy that only took ten minutes and only lasted three weeks.

Alex's new friends invited her out to eat burgers with them. They didn't know that she had just lost her job. All they knew were the grave injustices that her mother had perpetrated against her as a child and that she was really good at taking four shots of tequila in a row. Alex had $43 in her checking account, an amount she remained unaware of because she disliked checking her balance. Money, like the apocalypse and conservative government, remained a constant anxiety whose reality she was unwilling to embrace. When she saw the advertisement for the burger-eating contest listed in full color at the bottom of the menu, she wasn't thinking of her dwindling bank account or the liquidity of her finances. Rather, her decision was motivated by a particular type of hunger that only arose when she was trying to impress new friends. The hunger of leaving something indelible.

The deal was this: She had twelve minutes to eat a burger with two patties, three buns, topped with all the fillings, two onion rings and fries on the side. Should she finish, she would get the burger for free, a T-shirt, and her picture on the wall along with the other victors of the Egan's Bar and Grill Super Burger Challenge. If she failed, she would have to pay $22 and likely would vomit.

Her friends cheered when the server brought out the beast of the burger and set it in front of her. There was no way that she could finish it, they said. They underestimated Alex's power of destruction. She tore at the burger the way she wanted to tear at the flesh of her ex-girlfriend. She ripped it apart and stuffed it inside of her until there was nothing left. As a teenager she had often tried to make herself throw up in order to lose weight. It never worked. She could never trigger the gag reflex. She suspected she would be great at giving blow jobs though she had never given one and had no desire to do so. Why should she stuff her mouth with dick when she could fill it with dead cow covered in ketchup and mayonnaise and topped with lettuce, tomato, onion, and a smattering of pickles?

Many other burger competitors started to lose their strength when they reached the end of a challenge, but that was where Alex excelled most. She was never a person able to de-escalate any sort of situation and that included situations where she was stuffing huge amounts of food in her mouth. She found that burgers were always better in the end, when all the ingredients had lost their composure and were smushed together in a mass of mayonnaise and bun.

As the clock wound down and Alex moved onto the fries, her friends started cheering, pounding on the table in support. The other diners in the restaurant turned to look, expressing shock that someone so small was devouring a burger so large. They joined in on the cheer until the whole restaurant was shouting, enthralled by Alex's mastication. She had expected to feel like vomiting, she had expected the whole damn thing to come back up. Alex had never done anything in her life without it getting messy. She understood that it was necessary to wade around in the dirt for a while to get things done. Apparently, the only part of her that didn't want to revolt was her digestive tract, a system bent on keeping all that she put inside of it. She stood on the table as she took the last bite and the whole restaurant clapped and cheered. A baby in the corner started crying. Alex had never felt so full, probably because she'd never eaten a burger so large. Her friends were so impressed that they bought her drinks for the rest of the evening. It took a while for the alcohol to break through all that food to get to her blood stream, but eventually it got there. "Let's be friends forever," she said to her new friends. They weren't.

She was lucky it was summer when she was evicted from her apartment. County Fair season. Alex always complained that she was jinxed, cursed by some supernatural force that her atheist self didn't even believe in. For someone who was hexed, Alex was often quite lucky. "Bullshit," she said when she got the eviction notice. She smashed all her plates on the floor. She had purchased them from a thrift store and they didn't match. She left her couch behind, her bed that didn't have a bedframe, and the broken kitchen table. She didn't mop the floor or wipe the baseboards. She smoked cigarettes and put them out on the carpet. She didn't get the letter saying she didn't get any of her security deposit back because she didn't have a forwarding address. She stayed on friends' couches until they weren't her friends anymore and then she found new friends and new couches. She ate at the fair.

There were many different types of fairs. State fairs, county fairs, neighborhood fairs. Almost all of them had some kind of eating contest. Alex, who struggled to apply to jobs and had dropped out of college three-fourths of a semester in, entered every eating competition she could find. When there wasn't one, she made one, betting various fair venders on the amount of food she could eat if only they gave it to her for free. She met a girl that worked at the French fry booth at a county fair and they fucked next to the fence surrounding the fairgrounds until the cops came and kicked them out and then they fucked in the house where the girl still lived with her parents. Alex didn't know that the parents lived there until she woke up naked on the couch in the morning with the parents peering into her face. After they kicked her out, she beat the previous year's champion in a sushi eating contest by eating 60 rolls in ten minutes. "That's less than ten seconds per roll!" her opponent cried. She won a year of free pies during a pie-eating contest as a school fundraiser and never went to the pie shop to collect any of her prizes.

She stayed on one friend's couch for a week until her friend called her a "slob" and "ungrateful" and kicked her out. "Many people have hurt me before you to make me this way," Alex screamed as she shut the door. She called another friend who didn't have a couch, but she did have a floor and the floor was good enough for Alex. She competed in a lo mein-eating contest and had come out the victor with a two-hundred-dollar check only to discover the next day that she had food poisoning and spent the day on the toilet alternating holes through which the poison emerged. As it turned out, her stomach was like the rest of her body, something that would always turn on whatever was sustaining it.

She started to become well known in the competitive-eating circuit, which like any other circuit was smaller and more sexually intertwined than expected. It took most people years to break into the crowd, proving themselves over a myriad of competitions and food groups. It took Alex slightly less than a year from when she first consumed that fateful burger. Alex, like the worm everyone was afraid had burrowed beneath their skin. She won a banana-eating contest and then stuck her finger inside one of the other contestants who moaned in pleasure and then excused herself to go take a shit. She won a thousand dollars from a crab leg-eating competition and then moved from the couch into cheap hotels. She could've afforded something nicer, but she liked complaining about the bugs and the pubic hairs that she found in the bathroom.

She wintered between a homeless shelter, cheap hotels, and the houses of various girls. She got a tattoo of a slice of pizza on her arm. A tattoo of the face of a girl shoving a hot dog in her mouth. She travelled to competitions around the United States and was supposed to go to one in the Bahamas, but she was unable to get a passport on time because she didn't have a secure address. "Addresses are a way to fuck the impoverished," said one of her girlfriends who lived in a refurbished mansion sectioned off into apartments. Alex lived in the refurbished mansion with her for a couple weeks. The residents shared a hallway bathroom and got angry with her clogging it up post-eating binges. "I have a lot of stuff I'm trying to get rid of," Alex said. "A lot of shit to wade through." They lit matches after her poops, but there was nothing that could neutralize such stench. At the end of the two weeks, Alex and her girlfriend broke up and it had nothing to do with shits and instead related to some flaw that her girlfriend implied in Alex's persona.

The worst night of winter came when Alex lost a wing-eating contest to some guy from Japan or Korea, the specifics of which were unimportant to Alex in the face of a loss. She had been counting on the prize money to pay for somewhere to spend the evening. Without the cash, Alex was both unable to pay for a hotel room and for the drinks that she consumed after her wing-eating loss. The spicy wing sauce seemed to have inserted itself within every crevice of her body and nothing tasted so much like defeat than that burn sneaking its way around her gums. When the bar closed at two in the morning Alex was kicked out by the bouncer, a large man that hoisted her up by the armpits and threw her out into the cold. "You don't know what I've been through," she said and pounded on the locked door. She ended up falling asleep with her pants down on the toilet of a 24-hour diner, woken up by the employees who were trying to get in to clean.

Alex checked into the psych ward again that spring and was kicked out when she tried to demonstrate her consuming skills to the other patients. Consuming that much food, they said, was a harmful behavior and would not be tolerated on the premises. They didn't need anyone to escort her away. She left on her own and took the bus downtown and ordered the burger of the original burger challenge. It seemed smaller than it had the first time. She finished it with minutes to spare. No one clapped or cheered. No one was there to support her. It was like eating anything or nothing. She realized that binge eating was only fun with an audience. The T-shirt and free meal seemed like such a meager prize. Her eating was worth so much more.

Alex was in a bad mood when she reached the pinnacle event of her career path, one that included stuffing as many hot dogs in her face as possible within ten minutes. She had once told a competitor that if she made it to the hot dog-eating contest, the big show, that she would be "so happy that nothing else in the world could make her sad." As it turned out, many things could make her sad and she cared more about the loss of her most recent girlfriend than she did about any career successes. She didn't feel the same passion she normally did when she started dipping those buns into the water. It wasn't until she noticed the wing man—not a man with wings, but the man who had beaten her in the wing-eating contest—siting several seats down that she developed her eating fervor and began stuffing dogs down her gullet faster than she ever had before. She felt herself on the verge of a win and at the same time, felt herself starting to choke. It was alarming to have such a basic function taken away by a tube of meat. Her face grew hot and red and someone shouted, "She's choking!" and one of the moderators picked up her body and squeezed, a hug tighter than any she had ever received before. The dismembered dog went flying through the air and landed on one of the spectators who said, "Gross, I'm keeping this forever as a collectible." Alex was elated to almost die and then live again until she realized that she had come in fifth in the great hot dog-eating contest. "I wish I had died!" she declared as the winners took the podium. She made herself feel better by following some of the spectators to a nearby tourist bar and eating one of them out in the toilet stall, another type of eating contest that she always won. "How did you get so good at this?" the girl in the toilet stall cried, Alex's head between her legs. Alex responded, "A lot of things have happened to make me this way," as she licked her engorged clit.

WILD BIRD FEED EMPORIUM

There were attempted break-ins more days than not. People were insatiable when hunting for a good deal. That's what it felt like: hunting. It was appropriate that Chris spent most of his time in a store meant for birds. He was taking literally the phrase "the hunter becomes the hunted."

He had always felt a certain paranoia when going to the bathroom, particularly at parties and other gatherings. Who knew what was going to emerge from the dark depths of his body? He preferred toilets that were out of the way, tucked into some dark hallway and only used when guests were over. It took some exploration to find the perfect receptacles in the mall. He drew maps on the back of old receipts. The pens didn't work well. Retail pens never worked well. It was more like scratching. He scratched maps onto the backs of old receipts.

He ruled out the toilets by the main entrances of the mall, those centers of filth and children and world-wide STDs decorated with streamers of toilet paper. He expected that when the world ended it would start like this: a man from some unpronounceable distant land who picked up some unpronounceable virus on the airplane and then wiped his grimy hands all over the first shiny American bathroom he reached. The mall toilet-seat virus that killed everyone. If only they hadn't felt such insatiable desire for clothing with no sales tax in one convenient building. If there was anything Chris understood after living in the mall, it was the nature of death.

The best bathrooms were in the bougie department stores. He didn't look out of place in these places, or at least that's what he told himself. He had stolen enough clothing to have a versatile wardrobe. He could be anyone with the right outfit. Yet he couldn't help feel like the sales associates could see the homelessness on his skin. They were able to tell that he had not taken anything but a sink-shower in weeks. His even greater fear was that the sales associates could see inside of him to his deepest desires and anxieties, particularly his desire and anxiety over finding an empty bathroom stall.

His missions became covert. He ventured out in the mornings before the lunchtime rush in order to purchase some sustenance. He was big into soft pretzels lately, but sometimes he treated himself to a cinnamon roll or what he liked to call mall-Asian food, which existed as a blend of the orient and grease. He had to go places where the service was quick, where he wouldn't be seen and carted away. This was the riskiest part of his day, when he had to sneak out and back into his emptied store and hope that no one would notice. He looked back and forth like he was crossing the street, the bodies of shoppers, the cars, clutching his bag of fast-food in one hand and his drink in the other. When there was an opening in traffic, he made his quick and careful dash back into the sanctuary of his store. Back into his nest of gathered clothing, the makeshift pallet that he had turned into his bed. Back to his safe space, which wasn't safe at all.

He hadn't always lived in a mall. He wasn't born there and raised by feral mall people. Chris hadn't known that feral mall people existed until he became one himself, their putrid existence surpassed only by the dreaded mall walker. Before he'd become a mall person he'd had what he considered a successful relationship with a girl who was pretty enough and they shared an apartment where there was art hung on the walls. It had never been his apartment though. One of Chris's main flaws was that he'd never been able to understand what was his and what wasn't his, and his girlfriend had made it very clear when she broke up with him and kicked him out of the apartment that it was not his and neither was she. Their break up coincided with a grim meeting with the management of the bird feed store where Chris worked who announced that they were closing all but three branches of the store, saying there simply wasn't the demand for bird feed in such a cold environment as Minnesota. Chris had just become manager the week before. He'd gone out to celebrate at the mall restaurant with animatronic animals where the food was bad, but he enjoyed the simulated thunderstorm that took place during their meal.

Chris stayed there until the end, helping pull down the shelves and selling bird feed marked down to fifty percent off and then seventy-five percent off and then nearly free. Even then their sales were slow. No one walked into a mall intending to buy birdseed and it was not an impulse buy. It didn't have the same shine and glamour as a five-dollar T-shirt. There were still piles of bags of bird feed lying in the store, but the cash register had been removed as the last valuable in the place. Once when Chris's levels of hunger had reached desperation he'd tried eating some of the feed and discovered once and for all that he was definitely not a bird. He was a man. He wanted a steak. He wanted some pizza rolls.

Chris had been staying on a friend's couch during the closing, but the friend had started dropping hints that it was time for him to go. Working in phrases in every conversation like, "When you get your own place" or "When you leave forever can you take out the trash?"

One of Chris's perks as manager had been that he was rewarded with a key in order to close and open the store. On the final day of the store closing he was the last one left. He sighed the kind of sigh that people make when they are about to leave somewhere forever, but he never left. That was the longest he went without leaving, staying in the store an entire forty-eight hours before he was sure his bladder was going to erupt and he ran out of the store to the nearest bathroom. That's when this whole obsession with the perfect mall bathroom started.

The store management had taken down the sign from the entrance, the one that said "WILD BIRD FEED EMPORIUM," but they had left all the sale signs covering the windows, advertising a sale that was both no longer happening and perpetually happening. The signs were his refuge as they covered giant glass windows and obscured him from sight. What he had failed to consider was that the sale signs drew tourists and mall shoppers. The lack of a labeling sign was not a deterrent, nor was the dark interior. The shoppers smelled a sale and they were determined to get at whatever it was. They pulled on the locked doors and peered in the slits between the signs.

"Hello?" they called, banging on the glass.

Some of them backed off when they figured out the doors were locked and from those shoppers Chris merely hid, closing his eyes until they went away. The larger majority though stayed, refusing to stray from their mission of hitting every store in the mall and perusing the best sales. They hit the glass until Chris was sure it would break. They hit the glass like he was an animal at the zoo they were trying to rouse.

"Are you open or what?" they yelled in their Midwestern accents.

When Chris could take it no more, he would go up to the doors and yell as loud as he could, "This is not a store!"

The shoppers would back off, alarmed that they had been yelling at an actual person rather than a conscious-less storefront. People will yell at anything they think is not alive.

Thus Chris had to be careful when he emerged from the store that he now affectionately referred to in his head as "the birdcage." Who knew what the shoppers would do, desperate for any sort of deal they could get?

He only allowed himself two bathroom breaks in a day, once to take a shit, something that no longer happened on the daily now that he only ate once a day and his meals consisted primarily of carbs, and once to shower or the closest approximation of it that he could manage. When attempting to take a shit he allowed himself the luxury of the second-story Nordstrom's bathroom, a bathroom he deemed the most luxurious bathroom in the mall, an award he would've made a placard for if he had any of the materials or clout required in the making of a placard. The second-story Nordstrom's bathroom had a couch, and after an extended toilet sit he would sometimes allow himself a brief couch sit if only to remember what it felt like to sit on a couch. Of all the things he missed of his civilian life, couch sitting was the most potent. Sitting on the couch was what made him feel human.

He was careful not to go to this bathroom too frequently. The sales representatives would start to recognize him and think he was one of those mall crazies. Chris knew he was distinctly different than the mall crazies, but could not define in what way. He wore different outfits. Sometimes he stole outfits with the express purpose of wearing them to the bathroom. Outside of a short period when he was fourteen, Chris had never been a shoplifter. When he moved into the mall, he shoplifted as a method of camouflage. People were less likely to recognize him if he dressed in different clothing. He shoplifted everything. Giant T-shirts with graffiti on them. Businessman button-ups. Hipster flannel. He could be everybody. He could be five people in one. He knew how to blend in. He knew how to not stand out in a crowd. He knew how to live in the mall and never be noticed by anyone.

Until one day, during one of his sink-shower trips, when he noticed a tiny dark female face in the bathroom mirror.

He only took sink showers at night long after the mall had closed. The only people in the mall at that time were security guards and people getting out of late-night movies. He had stolen a compact mirror from a high-end makeup store that he used to look around corners and check for the security guards. It made him feel like a spy. It disappointed him that he couldn't actually dress like a spy because someone dressed in all black late at night in the mall would be too suspicious. Instead he dressed in his "normal man" outfit of a sweatshirt and jeans. The department stores were locked at that hour and he was forced to go to one of the plebeian bathrooms. Still some were cleaner than others, and he liked to go to the one stationed by the dying music and DVD store and more niche clothing stores.

The mall got cold at night without any bodies to heat it. One of the more interesting facets of the mall was that despite being located in a cold weather region, the mall had no heating system and relied entirely on the heat of its patrons. How many bodies did it take for the mall to reach room temperature? Chris didn't know. On his pallet in the bird feed store, Chris slept under piles and piles of stolen clothing. He had not yet managed to steal a comforter. Something down and upscale.

He acted casual and relaxed on the way to the bathroom. He was unaware of the security systems in the mall, banking on the fact that they hadn't caught him yet. He walked in a manner that said he was the type of person who belonged in a mall in the middle of the night. If only he could steal a security guard uniform then he could have full run of the place. He was lucky that the bathrooms remained unlocked for the night. He didn't know what he would do if they started locking them. Probably start growing dreadlocks and a dirt layer of clothing.

He had stolen a bottle of obnoxiously scented body wash and overpriced shampoo. He washed one body part at a time with a bright pink loofa. It was a long process. He valued his cleanliness. He knew how filthy his birdcage would become if he ever stopped washing himself. He imagined mall security finding him covered in dirt surrounded by bags of shit. If they ever found him, he didn't want it to be like that. At the very least he wanted the newspaper headlines to read "EXTREMELY CLEAN MAN FOUND IN ABANDONED BIRD FEED STORE IN MALL."

He was washing his armpits when he saw her. His armpits became like nests in the daytime. He scrubbed until the hairs were foamy and let the suds run down his chest. She was watching this process. She was small and dark with bird-like features. She might not have had bird-like features, but since Chris spent several hours a day staring at bags of bird feed this was the only way he knew how to describe something. She was staring at his chest like she had never seen a man's breasts before.

"Who are you?" Chris said, worried she was undercover security. She turned and left the bathroom without a word.

After seeing her the first time, Chris couldn't leave his nest without a spotting. She was everywhere, at the pretzel stand, hiding behind racks of clothing that he was trying to steal. When he saw her, he ran or she ran. It was hard to tell who ran first. Chris ran until he couldn't see her anymore. He ran until he felt safely blended into the crowd of tourists and was able to return to his home.

"I am being followed" he scratched into one of the receipts for no one in particular. Writing down his thoughts helped him process them. At various points he had also written, "Victoria's Secret is an uncomfortable place for men." "Don't get the beef stir-fry from Panda Express." And "Hungry."

Still, no one came for him except the normal barrage of tourists banging on the doors. He slowly began to let his guard down like a bird at a bird feeder in a backyard with a dog. One day he left the mall entirely to steal a coffee table from the IKEA across the way. He stole the tools to put it together from the Sears in the mall. He swiped a portable DVD player on sale from Best Buy and lay on his pallet watching DVDs with headphones plugged in so no one could hear the noise. Out of boredom he managed to steal an entire tuxedo, which he wore around the birdcage for two whole days without taking it off because he felt so fancy. During all of these excursions, he saw her. Each time she wore a different outfit. Each time she looked surprised to see him, almost as though he were the one who was following her and not the other way around.

The second-to-last time he saw her was his last night in the mall. He didn't know it was his last night in the mall. He'd taken a break from his favorite sink-shower bathroom after he'd seen her there, but he was building up his courage again. No other bathroom had quite the charm or cleanliness of this bathroom.

She wasn't in there when he entered. He didn't hear her come up. She was noiseless in her movements. He was lathering up his back when she came in, trying to reach spots that his inflexible arms struggled to get. He jumped when she came up to him, alarmed at her sudden proximity. He didn't resist when she kissed him. It'd been so long since he'd touched anyone. They made love in the bathroom that night. Both of them covered in soap suds, both of their clothing with the tags still on them thrown on the floor.

"Who are you?" he asked again when they were done.

She said nothing, just left the bathroom and disappeared into the cold night mall.

The security guards came for him the next day. They had footage of him, they said. They had never witnessed such explicit acts performed on the bathroom sink before, they said. They had followed him from one camera to another all the way back to WILD BIRD FEED EMPORIUM. They had noticed him for months, they said, but were never certain where he was coming from. It was embarrassing, being dragged handcuffed through the mall like that. All of his stolen clothes bagged up and taken in for evidence.

"Evidence of what?" he asked. They had no answer for him.

He saw her again briefly as they pulled him out of the mall. She was wearing a dress he had never seen her in before. It was low cut and he imagined what she looked like without it. She was holding a soft pretzel in one hand and a soda in the other. She didn't wave. She just stared like everyone else in the crowd and then was swallowed up completely. At the station, he tried to ask who she was and if she was the one who turned him in, but they acted as though they didn't know who he was talking about. They let him take a shower in jail though and that was nice. He had forgotten what it felt like to have water rushing over his entire body at once. Like a birdbath on a hot summer day.

Fever

Cutting the body open, that had been her mistake, though it was only a large mistake in a series of smaller mistakes that had stemmed from an online dating site. In Kimberly's experience, most, if not all, incidents in life stemmed from online dating.

She loved him immediately. She had to love him immediately. In online dating there was no incubation period, no series of small hand holdings, no dancing near each other and then next to each other, no build-up of coffee, then dinner, then sex, and no conversation of "Oh, but we've known each other forever." In online dating, daters went in with the expectation that maybe they would love each other forever and get married and have children, which was a lot of pressure for people who had never really seen each other before. But they knew going in, knew from a series of questions and polls, buttons clicked, that they had the same goals and desires. They wanted the same number of children and they wanted to have sex the same amount per week and that was more than most people knew about anyone around them, more than they knew about anyone that they met casually at a party or through work.

They met at a bar. All she knew was that he was a white person with brown hair. With the exception of one date, every man she had met online had been a white person with brown hair. It was easy for her to imagine loving such a ubiquitous face. He would be wearing a gray T-shirt, he had texted her earlier. It had been a few days since he'd shaved his face and he had some stubble. He would be drinking a beer. "I will be wearing a red ribbon in my hair," she texted back. "So you know it's me."

Kimberly had meant to get to the bar first. Strategically place herself in a booth with a drink in a martini glass. Something delicate but lethal. She had, after all, listed fancy cocktails on her profile as one of her interests. But she was running late, her eyeliner smudged, and she struggled to find a parking spot near the bar and thus parked several blocks away. She had forgotten, it turned out, to wear the red ribbon. It didn't matter. He recognized her anyway, his neck craned toward the door with longing.

She knew that she loved him around an hour and fifteen minutes into that first date. This was not as romantic as saying love at first sight, so she still said love at first sight even though there was some breathing room between sight and love. They were talking about their favorite foods when she felt the confirmation of feelings. They both loved pasta and cheese and pizza. They loved it when restaurants had a bread basket. Peaches were their favorite food to eat in the summertime. Kimberly had never understood the insides of a man the way that she understood this man's insides.

The man had a steady job at a corporation in the city. There was room for advancement. He rented his own apartment. There was art hanging on the walls. The man was like an actualized version of what a man should be. On weekend nights, after they went out to dinner somewhere ethnic and affordable, they would curl up on his couch together. "This is perfect," she said. That was a lie. It wasn't perfect at all.

The man refused to turn on the heat, even in the middle of winter. Because he was a practical man, because he wanted to save money, because he wanted to plan for their lives together, he refused to turn up the thermostat. Kimberly would walk into his apartment and exclaim, "Cold!" and he would laugh as though coldness were not a real symptom of misery. Kimberly would suggest spending the night at her apartment and the man would always decline, saying, "Maybe another night" or "I need to get up early in the morning and it would be better for me to stay here," though Kimberly also needed to get up early in the morning and spent the night shivering in his cold apartment.

Despite this, she still loved him, and when he came down with seasonal influenza she brought homemade chicken noodle soup to his house and curled up next to his aching, sick body, which radiated a glowing heat. The man expressed some desire to be "left alone" claiming that he was "not in the mood to cuddle," but oh how Kimberly enjoyed that feverish body like a human-sized heating pad.

She was relieved when he was no longer sick and they could resume their normal activities of going out to dinner and the occasional movie, though she missed that other body, the warm one, so she stopped washing her hands and started deliberately rubbing herself in all sorts of things hoping that he would catch some germs that caused his body to broil. It surprised her how resilient the human body was, how little he wanted to get sick, though he did develop a persistent stuffy nose that leaked down into his throat that caused a cough that led to bronchitis and kept them both up at night.

Dirty bathrooms were not enough for the type of warmth that she wanted from this man, and so she took to the internet and started bidding on a variety of sweets that had been licked by small children with lethal viruses. Such sickness didn't come cheap. Kimberly had to sacrifice her vacation fund and part of her savings, but she wouldn't need a vacation when her man radiated warmth like the sun. They could take a staycation where she wrapped herself around his body and spoon-fed him chicken soup and their couch could be like a sandy beach and the shower like an ocean.

Because the man was the picture of health, he did not purchase candy for himself and instead only consumed sugar when the sugary items were placed in front of him. Though it would seem that this implied a great strength of willpower, it actually was the opposite, as the man was incapable of resisting any sort of candy product once it had entered his home and he had only learned not to buy any after consuming an entire bag of organic malted milk balls in a single sitting and then spending the rest of the evening throwing up those malted milk balls in the toilet. Thus, all Kimberly had to do was place the soiled sweets at strategic locations around the house and the man would put them in his mouth. He put them in his mouth without thinking or asking. He put them in his mouth like it was necessary to his survival. It hurt Kimberly's feelings a little that he never thought to offer her any or to ask her permission to eat all her candy, but at that point she knew that she was asking for too much.

The body can incubate an illness for several days without any sign of illness. Kimberly rubbed herself all over the man's body looking for signs of fever or contamination. The man, in return, was excited by how much she wanted to touch him and they had one of their most passionate love-making sessions yet. Perhaps sex would've been the more rational route to making their love warm.

When the sickness came it came with a headache and a cough, a full-body soreness that kept the man in bed with the exception of short bursts of nausea during which the man would flee to the bathroom only to have nothing come out. Kimberly tried to get close to the man, to throw her arms over his sweaty chest, to touch her cool palm to his forehead, but he told her no, he was too sick, he didn't want her to touch him when he felt like that and she lamented giving him such a virulent virus and vowed that the next time, the next time she made him sick like that, she would make him less sick so that his only symptom would be a pleasant warmth throughout the body.

It was unexpected when she returned home from work with a bagful of herbal Chinese flu remedies and cans of chicken soup that she found his body cold. She didn't even notice at first, peering into the room to smile at him before unpacking the groceries in the kitchen. It was only when she tried to get him to swallow several of the flu remedy tablets that she realized that he couldn't swallow or speak or move at all because he had passed away while she was at work. She had only been gone for eight hours and yet already his body was cold and she was sad, so sad, that she had missed his ultimate peak of warmth and that's when she decided to take the butcher's knife and slice his body open and crawl inside. She couldn't even fully encapsulate herself in the body because his ribcage was in the way and she didn't have enough strength to break all those bones and thus she lay on top of the corpse and cried and cried, because he was already so cold, and already so distant from the man who had once loved her.

His laptop was next to him when he died. Kimberly wiped away the organ juice from where it had leaked from his body and onto the keyboard. The warranty would never cover such a smudge, she knew. It was then she discovered that while the man was feverish, while he was too sick to move or cuddle that he had been talking to other girls on the online dating website. She had always assumed that he had rendered his account inactive as she had rendered her account inactive because they were in love, because it was possible that they were going to get married and raise two to three children together and get a large-breed dog. Instead, the whole time he had been talking to other potential women and there was no denying that it was a scandalous thing, men do not talk to women on online dating sites without wanting something. She left the man's body there, the hole in his chest leaking all over everything. Kimberly went home and reactivated her online dating site account. "Must be warm," she added to a list of requirements for her future man.

Plenty of Men Love Silent Women

He was only six years older than her, but he didn't know that. He didn't know what her bedroom looked like or what she ate in the mornings. He only knew the clasp of her hand, the weight of her body as he carried it over the ocean waves.

His contract had a lot of stipulations. He would need a dressing room. A plate of brie and crackers. Scalding-hot coffee with a shot of sugar-free caramel syrup. Makeup and wardrobe. A hot tub and a cold tub. They were to touch only when the paparazzi cameras were in sight. Adriana was not to look him in the eyes. She was never to speak.

Their first date took place at the entrance of a club. Adriana's topknot so tight that it seemed to be pulling on her brain. Eric took her hand, his fingers meaty. He was wearing sunglasses even though it was nighttime. His jeans were ripped in a purposeful manner. They walked into the club with cameras flashing and they didn't smile because smiling wasn't how celebrities indicated they were in love. Once inside, he disappeared behind a curtain. So much stealth for a body with such muscle. Adriana's publicist pulled her to the bar where she was given cranberry juice because alcohol was bad for the skin. She took the requisite number of photos with her fans. Most of them didn't know who she was yet, but were eager to be involved with any sort of celebrity. The clout of being able to claim knowledge of a person before they were famous.

Adriana collected tabloids in a three-ring binder filled with clear plastic sheets. Watching herself become famous was like watching a distant childhood acquaintance become famous. She was happy and simultaneously jealous of the person in the pictures who was both her and not her at all. Previously, her appearances in these magazines had been minor. A tiny nod on the red carpet. Something stolen from one of her social media platforms. When she was next to him, she made the cover. There was a feeling she'd anticipated when she finally saw herself there that never fully arrived. No fireworks inside the heart, no celebration with girlfriends over a bottle of champagne. There she was on the cover and the next week, something different and she was forgotten. What a thrill and a disappointment to learn that her dreams weren't what she wanted after all.

They went to the beach for their second date. They arrived separately. Eric in a SUV, the windows darkened and Adriana riding shotgun in her publicist's Honda Fit. Her hairstylist arranged her red hair in natural-looking beach waves. Remember, they said. You are not to speak.

Eric looked like a Greek god or an underwear model when stripped down to his swimsuit. A body entirely devoid of fat. She didn't know there were so many ridges that could be hidden beneath the skin. His chef laid out some sausages on a grill that wasn't hot and the paparazzi snapped photos of Adriana standing next to it. They took a picture of her with a hot dog in a bun, held up to her lips, almost touching. People liked it when celebrities ate because they felt as though it gave them justification for their own indulgences. What they didn't realize is that she didn't put the food in her mouth, that the dog and the bun were abandoned in the sand for the seagulls who ate greedily, preferring her cold sausage to anything that they could find in the sea.

Assistants stood around with tiny brushes to wipe the sand off Eric's glistening body. He posed on the shore. An Adonis on the contemporary earth. She knew, as they all knew, that such perfection wasn't obtained naturally and was aided by steroids and starvation. No one tested the actor to determine the authenticity of his hotness. It was his job, after all, to make it appear real.

They wanted them to pose in the ocean. The beach had been cleared for their arrival. Carcasses of dead fish swept away, remnants of other humanity removed from the shores. The privilege of loneliness. Should they have wanted, they could've arranged for a seemingly emptied earth.

No one asked if she could swim and she didn't tell them otherwise. This was what she had been taught on set: never say no. The salt, she figured, would keep her buoyant until she returned to shore.

The water was cold, its mass too great to be warmed by the sun. She wondered how it would feel to be so impenetrable. Just dive in, they said. We want it to look like you are having fun.

The current felt like a hand on her ankle, so purposeful in its malicious dragging. Entering the sea was the closest she'd ever become to being eaten alive. She could only imagine the places she would go when it swallowed her completely. It was then that she considered the consequences of an all-juice diet. There were, after all, arguments as to why the body needed calories to survive and the weakness of her limbs made itself clear as she was swept out to sea. She wondered, in the moments before she blacked out, if her death would make the tabloids. Her own cover, finally.

Adriana didn't remember being rescued, didn't remember Eric pulling her out of the water as though he was playing the role of a superhero. There were pictures of him carrying her, Adriana's long red hair dangling across his muscled arms and her body, limp and lifeless. He kissed her awake back on the seashore. It turned out later that he didn't even know CPR. He was performing an imitation of the CPR he had done in movies and that performance turned out to be as effective as the real thing. She opened her eyes and there he was, like a tabloid on this earth.

She opened her mouth. She started to speak. "I," she said and then it trailed away because nearly dying didn't negate the stipulations of the contract. Eric left her there, still coughing up water, to eat the brown rice and chicken that he was fed on a strict schedule. Nutrients, he said, waited for no one.

She didn't love him then, not yet, not any more than the ordinary way that people love those that have saved them. It seemed fruitless. Such men were always surrounded by a swarm of women, music-video girls and Victoria's Secret models. She was beautiful, but her beauty was inoculated by the beauty of others. There were a billion women like her. So many fish in the sea.

As a subject of tabloid fodder, she knew the types of falsehoods they printed. Nonexistent pregnancies and unconfirmed marital troubles. Secret affairs based off a handshake or a business lunch. Just because they told untruths did not mean it was all false. All rumors started somewhere. All lies at a polarity from the truth.

The cover of the tabloid was a picture of him carrying her. They had brightened the hue of her hair until it was red like a marker and cut off part of her ribcage. Adriana didn't mind having pieces sliced off. No matter how thin she became there was always more to lose. Her skin looked pale as though she had emerged from the deepest part of the ocean, as though he had found her there living in a sea cave with her fish friends.

IN LOVE?!?!?! the cover said and inside zoomed into a close-up of his face looking into hers. She had never seen him like that before, from the outside looking in. Adriana had never gotten any radiation of love from Eric directly, love like the feeling she got when she stood too close to the microwave. Perhaps, though, her sensors had been turned off. She was discounting the allure of her lifeless pale body as he carried it through the waves. For in the picture, there was no doubting his love, no questioning the realness of what was portrayed. His eyes, like a dog, wet and pleasing.

Instead of putting the picture in her binder, she cut it out and had it framed and hung it on the wall next to her bed. It was expensive, but she justified the cost with the potential earnings she was going to get for being connected with him. Eric, his skin shining like armor, watching over her as she slept. How comforting it was to have a savior and one so photogenic at that. How different it would have been had she been saved by one of the camera men, uniformly fat and ugly.

Adriana wanted to leap into Eric's arms the next time she saw him, but she couldn't because her heels were too high for leaping and her dress too tight for any sort of spreading of her legs and she had a contract that forbid such things. They were at an awards show. Eric was nominated for his role as a supporting actor and Adriana was there to accompany him. Now that she knew that he loved her, each of his movements took on a different meaning. The clasp of her hand as they walked down the red carpet. His mutterings about the celebrities strolling around them. She realized, for the first time, that he hadn't forbidden her from speaking out of disdain, but rather because he loved her too much to hear anything at all. Her voice, exposing their relationship for what it was, an undying passion.

There were pictures of her glancing up at his face in wonderment. Pictures of them, his arm around her waist. A kiss. An interview where he said, "I have everything that I could ever want. I'm at the point in my life where I want to settle down." The thing about starting a relationship wordlessly was that it made it easier to read what was never said. It was starting to feel comfortable, their silence. No room for arguments or discussion. They agreed on everything because there wasn't anything else.

Adriana knew that the damage she was doing to her walls was going to come out of her security deposit. She figured that once she got her big movie deal then she would buy someplace. Maybe something near the ocean. Eric, she figured, would move in eventually. It was hard to determine such deadlines in a relationship when they avoided difficult subjects and talking at all. Meanwhile she clipped the photos that grew increasingly common. Them at the awards show, them at a restaurant, an uneaten burger on her plate, them seen walking by his condo in Malibu. Chips of paint fell to the floor where she pounded nails into the wall. She didn't bother cleaning it up. She was going to hang pictures until the entire wall came crumbling down.

"You know it's not real," her publicist said. Adriana had gotten a small tattoo on her arm that said, "I love you," that she flashed to Eric each time she felt that burst of emotion. He responded by wearing a shirt that said, "I love A.M.," which most definitely meant, "I love Adriana Meer." Adriana told her publicist that she had been working in Hollywood for too long and could no longer tell the difference between real and fake. "Just because we were set up doesn't mean it's not destiny," she said.

She found his address by searching through her publicist's records. Adriana had been to Eric's house, but it wasn't his real house. It was the house that the paparazzi thought he lived at that he accessed through a secret tunnel from his actual house. There were houses and then there were places that served as fronts for where people really lived. Only the people that really knew Eric, like Adriana, were able to break into someone else's computer and steal his address.

She was banned from speaking with Eric, which certainly was different than writing Eric. She still worried that she would get in trouble and that his agent would tell her agent that she had broken the stipulations of the contract and she would be fired from her position as his lover and she would be thrown, metaphorically speaking, back into the sea. She didn't use her own handwriting and instead cut letters from the tabloids of their love. WhY CAnT WE JuST Be tOGEThEr mY LovE.

They got together in a private room at a restaurant, just them, their entourage, and the paparazzi because Eric's team was worried about penetration. His address had been leaked, they said. They did not yet known how far the damage had spread. They couldn't leave Eric vulnerable to all those that wanted to eat him alive, both literally and not.

Adriana loved being included in this inner circle. Receiving her salad and having it taken away after she had eaten her allotted tomato. Her fish with a side potato that she wasn't allowed to touch. A flaming dessert that burned until there was nothing left. Eric was so much better than her previous boyfriends, men that brought Adriana back to their apartments just to fuck. Her manager who liked to press his body against her body and say, "Oh, I bumped into you," who one time hissed in her ear, "If you ever try to sue me, I will ruin you." Eric never touched her without asking. Eric never touched her without clear orders from the camera crew.

Adriana landed a role as a superhero in a crew of superheroes in an upcoming movie. She was to play Data Babe, a girl that could hack into computers with her mind. The role involved a lot of intense staring off into the distance. It was the biggest role that she had ever had. It broke her heart that Date Babe was in a different universe than Eric's reoccurring role as Shark Boy, a man that could grow sharp teeth and gills at will. She wanted them to save the world together, one tight bodysuit at a time.

It came as a shock when her publicist called to inform her that she and Eric had broken up. Their relationship had run its course and was no longer interesting to their fans. Eric's superfans still needed to believe that there was a chance to earn his love. Adriana didn't eat for three days, which was a day longer than her previous record. Her publicist told her that she looked great when she showed up for her Data Babe fitting.

Adriana drank some cocktails with her girlfriends. Cocktails that were actually just cranberry juice and girlfriends that were other emerging actresses that were represented by her people. They got hors d'oeuvres for the table that the paparazzi ate after they left. Adriana wasn't drunk, but she was acting as though she was. She got in her car and drove erratically. If she had been in a movie, she would've driven off a cliff, taking Eric with her as she fell.

Because she wasn't in a movie she drove to Eric's house. Eric's real house. His dogs ran up to greet her as though she was a stranger, because she was. Adriana wasn't afraid of the dogs because she knew the worst thing they could do was rip her to pieces and that wouldn't be any worse than the way that she already felt.

Eric had a very expensive security system that appeared to have missed his first floor bathroom window. Eric's house, unlike her tiny condo, had clearly been decorated by an interior decorator, someone who loved shades of beige. It was a disappointment to find that his bedroom wasn't decorated with tabloids of the two of them the way that hers was. She had imagined the two rooms to be a mirror image. Instead, his room was sparse. When she pushed a button on the wall, a TV emerged from the floor and flames burst from the fireplace.

Adriana looked very good when she was naked. Some people sacrificed themselves for the good of humanity or to achieve physical feats never before conquered. Adriana sacrificed herself so that she would look good naked, which was why she stripped down and arranged herself on Eric's bed. She wanted their first one-on-one meeting to occur while she was at her best.

She expected that Eric would come home shortly. In one of the tabloids, she had read that he was a homebody. This, amongst other things, turned out to be a lie. She lay on his bed for so long that her stomach started to grumble and her legs started to cramp. She thought about moving, but didn't want him to come across her in anything but her sexiest pose. She knew which pose was her sexiest because she had been filmed in many different poses and had studied these films intently until she knew herself better from the outside than she did in.

Her legs fell asleep and then her arms. All of the blood in her body pooled in a lake at her core. Crusts began to form at the corners of her eyes. Adriana worried about the integrity of her eyeliner. For the first time, she began to resent Eric and how he made her perform her love. She would tell him her feelings, she decided. After he came home and found her and they had sex.

It wasn't Eric who found her. Adriana knew as soon as she heard the laugh. All the girls did the same audition circuit, worked with the same people. All the girls were friendly and also hated each other. They knew that to the general populous they appeared as carbon copies of one another, thin with long flowing hair, but knew in their hearts that they were an individual and they, out of all the others, should be the one to achieve fame.

Katy was tall and blonde and Adriana had mocked her blandness. She was too much girl-next-door, too much second-best-cheerleader, the friend in a group of friends. How hurtful it had been when Katy had been cast before she was. How annoying when the tabloids had caught Katy on the street committing acts of goodness for her fans.

Katy had never played a villain in a movie, which showed just how great the disconnect was between screen and reality. She laughed like someone evil and she pulled a knife out of her pocket like someone evil too.

"Poor, Adriana," she said. No one even talked like that, like a comic-book villain that was made bitter and had spent years of their life clawing their way into power. "You believed the stories, didn't you? You thought Eric loved you even though the whole time he was really in love with me." Katy was wearing a man's button-down shirt that only looked good on her due to her slenderness. Adriana was trying to wriggle her limbs awake and was filled with the tingling sense of the veins refilled with blood.

"Why weren't you together then?" she asked. The sound of her voice surprised her. Since she had started dating Eric, she had talked less and less until she rarely spoke at all.

"People can't just be together because they love each other, Adriana," Katy said. "There are other things more important in this world than love like appearances and money." Adriana couldn't disagree with any of that logic.

Adriana tried to stand up as Katy was getting dangerously close with a large knife, but her feet were still asleep and she promptly fell over. "Open your mouth," Katy said and Adriana did because she was very amenable to taking orders. She was not expecting Katy to cut out her tongue. What a shock it was to have something that was once inside of her body on the outside. To see Katy standing there with her tongue in her hand, rendering her infinitely speechless.

The blood had returned to Adriana's limbs, though she still tingled. "You better leave," Katy said. She seemed unconcerned by the deep red stains on her shirt. As Adriana left the house, this time through the door, she heard the sound of the juicer turning on and perhaps, distantly, the sound of her tongue as it was drained of her fluids. "You can't even get all the nutrients that way," Adriana wanted to scream, but couldn't, because she couldn't scream anything and her mouth was full of her blood.

Adriana went to the doctor who told her that their tongue replacement technology hadn't advanced enough to replace what she had lost. She cried silently at her loss. She really was quite beautiful when she cried and the doctor patted her on the back for an inappropriately long time and wiped her face with tissues as though she had also lost her hands.

It was difficult to tell her agent and publicist what had happened because it was difficult to tell anyone anything. She had to drop out of her role as Data Babe. Everyone was very upset, but her agent comforted her and said, "Don't worry, plenty of men love silent women."

Skinny Girls Get Devoured Quickly

He was divorcing his wife. Everyone knew this. Everyone knew this before he knew this. Tabloids are like tea leaves or fortune tellers. They tell the future and no one believes them until it happens. I didn't believe it was going to happen because I was stuck on this ideal of love. I wanted to believe that two people who had been in a movie together could fall in love and buy a house worth twenty million dollars and have two perfect children and love each other forever. As it turns out, they could do all of those things except the forever part. Forever turned out to be nine years, which I guess is a long time when you're used to love that lasts for the entirety of a two-hour movie.

He wasn't present during the hiring interview. I don't know if he ever saw my résumé. He didn't know about my brief stint as a fast-food worker or the ten months that I spent folding clothes at a Macy's. It was better that he didn't know those things. It wasn't like I expected us to fall in love or anything, but I joked about it with friends. I joked about a lot of things with friends. He didn't hire me for my looks. He wouldn't have hired me for my looks anyway. I was twenty pounds overweight and recovering from some mysterious rash that was probably caused by stress. I wasn't going through an easy time in my life either.

I saw her once, the ex. She was wearing sweatpants and sunglasses. This was how I recognized her. She wore sweatpants and sunglasses every time she didn't want to be recognized. It was like a uniform. Despite her claims that "she loved to eat pizza" and she was "a big eater," I could see her bones through her baggy clothing. I didn't know that the human body had so many bones. I got a D in high school biology. It was possible that she had been crying, but it was hard to tell with the sunglasses. Her skin was looking blotchy. She ignored me. I don't know if it was so much that she was ignoring me or that she didn't see me at all. My body was like the background to her.

He had a whole crew of maids. That's what he called us, "his crew," which was his way of saying he didn't know most of our names. He liked boat analogies and owned several boats that he kept in the giant garage despite living several hours from the ocean. A lot of the maids were from other countries. Mexico, Puerto Rico, Croatia, all over the place. I learned to speak a lot of Spanish and tidbits of Eastern European languages that way. We lived in the guest house that was a short walk from the main house. The way it was designed it was obvious that it was never meant for guests at all and guest house was just a nice word for "servant's quarters." There were four of us in a room together. We slept on bunk beds. It reminded me of that one semester of college that I attended. Some of the girls had been there for years. They had been there for so long that they remembered when a different celebrity lived in the house. When I asked them about this, they shrugged and said, "You know rich people, they're all the same."

We were like a family out there in the guest house. On weekends we would go out to the club together. We would joke that we were going to find a man who lived in a house like he lived in and sometimes we did. It never happened to me specifically, but on occasion one of the maids would flirt with a real rich guy and he would take her back to his mansion. She would think "this is it, my future is set," but then he would never call her and it would turn out that he had some skinny wife who was just vacationing at a spa somewhere. He never knew that we went out like that. He thought that we were docile, like cows.

You would think having a big nice house like that and all those maids would mean this his house was spotless. Let me just say that he had all those maids for a reason. The ex-wife had steadily purchased dogs throughout their marriage. I think she was trying to fill the lack of love he gave her with puppies. These dogs were all purebred, real nice looking dogs, but she never trained them. They didn't want to install a doggie door on one of the many doors in the house, because the doors were "unimaginably expensive." When the dogs wanted to shit and they often wanted to shit, they did it all over the carpets, which were also "unimaginably expensive." Half of our job as maids included picking up the little poops left around the house by dogs with impeccable genetic backgrounds. It was optimal to reach the little shits before they invaded the rugs on an internal level, but often it was too late and we would be scrubbing those expensive foreign rugs and wood floors made of nearly-extinct trees for hours.

The first time it happened, I wasn't expecting it. How does a person expect that sort of thing? I was in the hallway before the fourth and fifth bedroom. I don't know what he was doing back there. I didn't even know he was in the house. I thought he was out of town for some movie or something. Later I would learn that he had been cut from the movie that day and replaced by somebody younger with more muscles.

He grabbed me in that hallway. I say grabbed like he lifted me and slammed me against the wall, but I was really too heavy for that. It was more like a gentle shove against the wall. He didn't even know my name at that point. I know because he asked me later, after we made love in one of the bedrooms. A couple of the dogs were in there with us. They stood there watching and wagging their tails and started barking as he came inside of me. I wasn't on birth control, but he didn't ask. It didn't occur to him to ask about that sort of thing. There was a cockroach crawling on the wall. The whole time we were having sex, even though my body was filled with a deep and endless pleasure, I kept wanting to get up and kill the cockroach. It put a little bit of a damper on my enjoyment.

After it was over he asked me some things about myself. I asked him some things about himself as well, but it felt like a front because I already knew everything. Everything there was to know was listed on the internet and in magazines. He told me about his hometown in Wyoming. It was almost the exact same transcript from an interview he gave in *STARRRR Magazine*. I smiled and nodded like I had never heard it before. As I was putting my maid-pants back on he asked me not to tell anyone about this.

"The other women will resent you," he said.

"I won't tell," I said. It felt like a scene from one of his movies.

All I wanted to do was go tell the other girls what happened. Brag about my sexual exploits the way that they bragged after the club. But he was right, they would be jealous and those girls were like my family. I didn't want something like sex to get in the way of our friendship. I stayed quiet, though I thought of the sex as I scrubbed the eighth bathroom floor and as I polished the fourth set of dishes. I thought of it as I lay in my twin bed that night, my big feet poking off the end. I told myself that it didn't mean anything. It was just sex. But I imagined moving into the main house and getting a big ring and acting all surprised when he presented it on one knee, even though I wouldn't be all that surprised because I saw a picture in a tabloid from when he proposed to his last wife and I knew exactly how he looked kneeling down like that.

There was one movie that he starred in where he was in love with this girl, but he didn't realize he was in love with this girl because she was really smart and wore glasses and he didn't fall in love with women like that. Halfway through the movie she gets laser eye surgery, only the surgery goes bad and she is blinded. He goes to visit her in the hospital and when he sees her lying there helpless, he realizes what a terrible mistake he has made and has to spend the rest of the movie making up for his poor behavior in the beginning of the film. In the end, he proposes on a boat and they get married and she quits her job to spend more time with him and she starts a charity for people blinded by laser eye surgery. I ate a lot of popcorn during the movie and got terrible heartburn afterwards, which sort of tempered my feelings on the whole thing, but I would say it was an okay film.

The second time it happened with him it was less sudden. It was almost as though he had been searching for me, examining all the corners of the house until he found me on the patio waxing his surfboard.

"Meet you in the back bedroom," he whispered seductively.

It would've been even more seductive if I knew what he meant by "back bedroom." There were at least five back bedrooms and I tried to think of which one was the most back, but ended up searching three or four of them before I found him posing naked on the bed. He had a lot of muscles. During intercourse, I spent a lot of time feeling them. They felt hard and plastic. They didn't feel like they should be part of the body at all. I wondered if he was actually part robot like in that one movie he starred in. He spent a lot of time touching my skin, grabbing at my curves and bulges. It was like he had never touched a real woman before. Like he had spent all of his time playing with Barbies and he marveled at the real thing.

While we were doing it, I happened to notice a crack in the paint on the wall. It must've started out real little, but already it was starting to spread. I thought to myself, "he needs to have this room repainted" and I thought about bringing it up, but it would've been a weird thing to say with his penis inside of me.

After it was over he again told me not to tell anyone.

I thought, "How are you supposed to take me out to dinner at a fancy restaurant if nobody knows about us?"

I worried I was smiling too much. The head is not a transparent place, but I felt as though it was. I worried the other women could see inside my head to all the dirty, inappropriate positions that we had put our bodies in. If they knew, they would call me a traitor.

It started to get hard to focus on work. I was constantly keeping an eye out for him lurking around the corner, waiting to ravish me. I made excuses to clean in parts of the house where I thought he would be. I threw fits when I was told to clean elsewhere. I placed myself like a statue, directly in his way. The problem was that there were a lot of large statues in the house and I wasn't made out of any type of marble.

I had placed myself in the way when I first saw them together. I recognized her of course. That blonde hair, that infamous haircut. I used to joke that I loved her. I said things like "I would sleep with her" even though I'm straight. People are willing to put aside their sexual orientation for celebrities in magazines. But when I saw her there in person, his arm around her little back, his lips on her skinny lips, I had never hated anyone more. Not the obnoxious teenage pop star, not the wife-beating singer. I knew that this woman, all 95-pounds best-beach-body of her, was the devil incarnate.

Early on in her career, before she was the famous waif who starred in superhero movies, she played the leading role in a low-budget horror film. I don't watch a lot of horror films, but I happened to catch this one as I was lured in by the misleading title, *The Bond*. I thought it was a movie about love, but instead it was a movie about demons. It started the way that all movies about demons start. A young couple moves into their new house that they have spent all of their life savings on and they are very happy. The man is a novelist and the wife is a wife. Two nights into their stay, they realize that their love nest is actually a demon hive and all of the demons seem to want to possess the wife. They cannot abandon the house because all of their life savings are tied up in the house and if they were to leave they would barely even be able to afford a hotel. The wife tells the husband it's fine, they'll stay. She can deal with the demons. What the husband doesn't realize is that his wife has already been possessed by several demons and she wants him to stay in the house so that he can impregnate her with demon babies. The husband eventually realizes that his wife is not herself and is, in fact, several demons and hires an exorcist. After a long and gruesome exorcism, the husband thinks all the demons are expelled and writes a bestselling novel about the experience. They live happily ever after, his wife heavy and glowing with pregnancy, until one day he finds out that there is still a demon left inside his wife and it is the biggest, baddest demon, and the demon eats his heart out of his chest and the wife gives birth to a demon baby. I understand that many parts of the movie are fictionalized. For instance, I know that the husband was not actually a novelist nor as handsome as the actor that played him. But in that moment, as I watched that woman on the couch with my man, I knew that she was possessed by a demon.

At one point she got up to use the bathroom. She never noticed me standing there, watching them with my broken heart. She also failed to notice a piece of dog shit on the floor and she stepped right in it with her expensive heels. I imagine she smelled like poop for the whole evening, but I never got close enough to take a whiff.

Their relationship came out in the tabloids the next day. Some paparazzo hiding in the bushes shot a picture of her leaving the house late in the night. I told myself they didn't sleep together, but the next day when I was cleaning I found a condom wrapper. I couldn't focus on my pain for too long though, because that's when I noticed that a colony of ants had infested the house and were proceeding to march around like they owned the place.

"Little fuckers," I said as I sprayed the room.

After watching so many movies, I had a very good understanding of love. I knew that if I really loved him then I needed to make a grand gesture to get him back. I tried several subtle tactics at first. I left roses out on the table that cost me half my week's salary, but I couldn't put my name on them in case the other girls noticed and he didn't even look at them anyway. I bought new lingerie that I wore underneath my maid uniform and hoped he would take off my maid pants again to look. He never did. I then decided to take some inspiration from the exorcist priest in the horror film, but rather than performing some weak and ineffectual exorcism I was going to kill the bitch.

I had never killed anyone before. I'm not a psychopath. I've seen a lot of movies with psychopaths in them and I am definitely not one. I have never worn someone else's skin on my own body or made furniture out of bones. I decided the easiest way to kill her would be with poison. Unfortunately there weren't any bottles lying around with a skull and crossbones on them to indicate that they could kill somebody and I was forced to get creative. I had read an article in the newspaper once about a lady who killed her husband with eye drops. Each day she put a few squirts in his coffee and eventually he just up and died. She was caught of course. The spouse is always suspected first in these sorts of cases or at least they are in movies. The only problem was that I didn't want to also poison him. There was no point in killing her if he wasn't still alive. I decided the best place to plant my poison was in the row of coconut water bottles that lined the refrigerator. Certainly a man wouldn't drink coconut water. I opened them carefully and squirted some eye drops in hoping that she would consume enough to make her die. When I resealed the cap I dabbed a little glue on the lid to make it seem like it had not already been opened and tampered with.

The next time she came over I was cleaning mud off his mountain bike in the garage. Her driver pulled up in a giant SUV with tinted windows. She got out of the car wearing this ridiculous outfit that only a celebrity would wear. Her pants were leather or fake leather probably because I think she was an animal activist. They sagged weirdly at her crotch. Her shirt was big and flowy and looked like it was made for someone twice her size. Over the flowy shirt she wore a flowered scarf that was tied loosely. I don't know why she needed a scarf, it wasn't a cold day. Despite this, she still looked flawless. I have never looked as good as she looked on that day and I almost felt bad that she had to die.

I wasn't working that night, but I hung around to watch the action. She drank at least one bottle of coconut water and two glasses of wine. She barely touched her food. She didn't seem sick, though it's hard to tell with those bulimic types whether they are sick or not. She was probably used to that feeling of nausea rising in her stomach. They shared a dessert after dinner. The way she took those tiny bites and ate them so slowly and felt her stomach afterwards as though the fat were already creeping up on her. I took some pleasure in her inability to enjoy chocolate. I ate an entire bar by myself before going to bed. It was hard to get to sleep that night. I had so much anticipation.

I expected there to be some sort of ruckus during the night. A cry for help. Someone screaming, "Quick! Call 911." I had never been in an emergency situation before, but I had seen a lot of movies that featured emergency situations so I was almost an expert. None of that happened. I slept soundly through the night.

There was nothing for me to do except continue my normal cleaning duties. He wanted us to rearrange his collection of sunglasses and pick out the five best pairs for his upcoming vacation. They were a mess, all just piled up in a drawer. Without us he would've been hopeless. It took three women most of the morning to do the job. In the afternoon I decided to walk some of the dogs. None of them were very good on the leash, but I felt bad for them being cooped up in the house all day with no attention. I understood those feelings. None of the dogs pooped on the walk. It was as though they were trained to go all over those expensive carpets.

She didn't come over that evening. I was grateful for that. I hoped that something embarrassing had happened like the eye drops had caused her to shit herself or something. I hoped that in some small way I had caused their demise.

I didn't see her again until three days later when she was found with bugs ravaging her body in the sixth bedroom. It was like an insect house in there. Cockroaches, ant, centipedes, spiders. Everything was trying to get a piece of her. That fat, like baby meat, fed only by the most organic of greens and purest of juices. They sucked it all out of her. By the time she was found there was almost nothing left. Skinny girls get devoured quickly.

The police came and did a full investigation. The paparazzi were everywhere. I tried to get in as many shots as I could. They would scream at me, "Lady, move," and I wouldn't because it was my house too.

It was a bullet that killed her. No one had heard a gunshot. They must've used a silencer. I have never held a real gun, but silencers are what trained killer use in movies when they don't want anyone to hear.

During the investigation the police discovered the whole house was booby-trapped. There was poison in the coconut water, poison in the food, a knife found in the library, four separate guns with unidentified owners. They held him, my precious baby, for a few days before letting him go. That's when they turned to us, the maids. They tried to get us to turn on each other. Asked who laid the traps and poured the poison, but we were too loyal to each other for that.

When asked about the motive, if we had worked together or separately, we each furrowed our brows and said, "What? Do you think this was some sort of elaborate plot? I loved him, that was all and she was trying to take him from me," and then proceeded to describe each room where he had made love to our bodies. Each place where he had pushed us up against a wall. Every speck of dirt we saw while he was doing it.

Needless to say they did not lock us up together or we would've probably killed each other too once we found out that he was having sex with everyone. I feel embarrassed at the weakness of my plan and wish I had chosen something greater, flashier, a bigger sign of my love. To kill someone for your love. That is the grandest gesture of all.

My stomach is getting bigger. I can't tell if it's from all the chocolate I am eating or if he impregnated me when he came inside of me in that back bedroom. When I lie in my cell at night, I think of the way he grabbed me. My skin like something precious. My skin that can contain something more than bones.

I pat my belly. I wonder what's inside.

Things Inside of Us

Her french fries were waiting for her at the fast-food counter.
A double cheeseburger. A cup still empty, waiting to be filled with her
drink of choice. She was going to choose diet cola. She always drank
diet cola, it was healthier that way. But she had to do something about
the baby in the toilet. She couldn't just leave it there, though that
thought occurred to her. Washing her hands, wiping between her legs,
all that blood. It had felt like a ripping, the sound the same even, as
when fabric rips. Her stomach had been hurting for weeks and she
didn't know why. She had thought it was gas. She could feel it moving
around in there, the way that gas does with its little hands and feet,
pressing the sides of her organs, begging for her to allow its release.

The baby was wailing. She took it over to the changing table,
which was already unhooked from the wall. The table smelled like baby
wipes. Her baby smelled like shit. There might've been some of that in
there too. She flushed the toilet. It clogged, but she didn't work there,
so it wasn't her responsibility to fix it.

It was purple and dirty. She took off her sweatshirt and wrapped it inside. Her T-shirt was stained underneath. She walked out of the restroom and got her food from the counter.

"Can I get this to go, please?" she asked.

She left her drink cup. She didn't have enough hands to carry everything. She ate in the parking lot, her mouth dry. She carried it home in the sweatshirt, using the sleeves like handles on a bag.

"That sweatshirt's ruined now," she said. "Cost me forty dollars."

Some men catcalled her as she walked inside. She had to balance the baby on one arm in order to unlock the door. There was nowhere to put it really, amongst the piles. She was what you could call a piler, not messy exactly, but it would be messy if all those towers were to get knocked down. She put it on a stack of mail. It made some noises. She was hungry again and opened the refrigerator and ate a pickle. The pickle juice dripped down her chin, across her hands.

She changed her shirt; the last one was soiled. Put on her work pants; they were just sweatpants really.

She carried it on the bus, swiped her card but only once. Sat in one of the seats meant for the handicapped. A kid next to her blasted music out of his headphones. He had a hood over his head. Hood-lum. There was something about bus windows that made the world look grey. She pulled the cord. The "Stop Requested" sign lit up. She grabbed the ball wrapped up in her sweatshirt, stepped off the bus and onto the curb. There was something about bus stops that collected litter. She entered the windowless building. It could be a box just as easily as a building. She punched her punch card. She sat at her desk.

Put the sweatshirt on the floor, its contents leaking. She put on her headset. There was some wax on it. The script was in front of her. Sometimes they sold one thing and at other times something else. The folds of her sweatshirt kicked, gurgled. She dialed a number. They didn't pick up. She dialed another number. Every few weeks, they would get a new list. Until they got a new list, they dialed the same numbers repeatedly.

"Hello?"

"Good morning, ma'am. I'd like to talk to you about—"

There was a click, constant clicking.

A man answered the phone. He was watching a western. She could hear him chewing. He was very interested in the product that would both help him lose weight and regulate bowel movements. People made their way onto the list for all sorts of reasons, but primarily for past vulnerability.

It started to shriek. She didn't realize that it was shrieking until she removed the sweatshirt.

The man on the phone was threatening to hang up.

"I want you to listen to me," he said. "I need to be convinced of something."

She hung up the phone. This was against company policy. They were only permitted to hang up on phone calls when there was some sort of verbal abuse involved. Swear words of some kind.

It had become crusty. Flakes coming off every inch of skin. She took it in the bathroom and stuck it under the sink, dumping the sweatshirt in the trashcan. She scrubbed it off until it was mostly clean, some pieces of grime stuck on there so hard they could no longer be removed and had become part of its body.

"Baby." Language degenerates to a single word when faced with something small.

Her coworker peered over her shoulder. She was eighteen. She had large hoop earrings that she admitted she had purchased from the chain store in the mall that primarily catered to children.

"Is your baby all right?" she asked.

"Yeah, it just hasn't taken a bath yet. I'm giving it a bath right now."

"Oh."

She took it out from under the faucet, stuck it under the blow dryer for a few seconds and wrapped it in paper towels. She took it back to her desk, sticking the package down by her feet. She called the man back. He didn't seem to remember her calling previously and bought an entire case of pills. Her boss stopped by and told her to clean up that mess under her desk. "Sometimes when things get too messy, new life starts to form," he said.

After work, she got back on the bus and the driver made her swipe her card twice, which was expensive. At home, she put on a sparkly dress and wrapped it in a matching scarf. She put on red lipstick. Sprayed some body-spray that was supposed to smell like cucumber melon, but she had never smelled a cucumber like that before. She spritzed a little on the scarf too: it still smelled funny, not like a normal person at all.

She took the bus to her favorite club downtown, showed her ID at the door and they checked her scarf to make sure it wasn't a package full of drugs. She ordered some jag bombs at the bar. Went out onto the dance floor, tripping over her heels, but not so much that she fell down. A man came up behind her, rubbed his front into her back, handed her a shot. The scarf was wriggling; it was a dancer already.

She went outside for a smoke break. It started wailing through the fumes. She passed her cigarette off.

"I can't smoke this no more," she said. "My scarf is already starting to reek."

She went back in the club and placed it on a barstool, stomach down. The same man or maybe a different man started to dance with her.

"Let's go back to my place," he murmured into her ear.

"Only if my baby can come too."

"Baby, you can bring your baby anytime."

She went and got it from the barstool.

"You got your purse?" he asked. "Let me close out your tab."

They got on the bus. He swiped his card twice. They sat in the back of the bus. He slipped his fingers up her sparkly dress and inside of her. They made out, sticking their tongues down each other's throats. He pulled the cord. "Stop Requested" lit up. They got off the bus and walked into his building. He held the door for her, which was good because her hands were full. His apartment was the kind of apartment that men live in: nothing on the walls, a plain white comforter. She set it on the table. He pushed her back onto the bed, everything white.

"You feel real loose, what've you had up here lately?"

She could feel the wet on her legs. She thought for a second that it was his cum; that it was trailing out of the inside of her.

"Are you on your period?" he asked.

"No," she said.

He was still inside of her or it felt like he was, which were essentially the same thing. It started to cry on the table. There were tears on her face as well. The man's body was sweaty, a substance sticky like glue.

"When you said baby, I thought you meant something else," he said.

The mixture of cum and blood together had turned his sheets pink. It looked like tie-dye. She stuck her fingers in it, put them in her mouth.

There was a thump. She looked over; it had rolled off the table. The scarf sparkled on the floor.

"Too bad," he said. "Babies aren't supposed to be able to roll over this early. It would've been real smart."

Conjoined

The bab[ies] are born with an inappropriate amount of body parts.

Recorded: two heads, two arms, two legs, three lungs, two hearts, one uterus, one vagina.

Assumed previous conversation between the mother and father: "I just want them to be healthy. Ten fingers and ten toes."

Assumed opinion of the superstitious: "There was not enough specification."

The older theory is fission, the cell never splitting apart completely, together even in the womb. The newer theory is fusion, the cell splitting completely, but then finding like-features, merging back together again.

One uncle, now estranged, leans over the unit in the ICU and thinks (undocumented):

They should name one Circus and one Freak, so when they are called Circus Freak it won't be alarming."

Recorded past examples:

Mary and Eliza (allegedly): First documented case. Image recorded on cakes, later to be claimed as "just two poor women who weren't conjoined at all."

Chang and Eng, formerly of Siam: When asked what they were, they responded with, "We are Siamese."

Millie and Christine: Born slaves, originally referred to as "The Carolina Twins" and later changed to "The Two-Headed Nightingale."

Daisy and Violet: played themselves in the movie *Freaks*. Famous lines: "One of us." Daisy died first. Violet died between two and four days later.

Lori and Dori, later Lori and George. George is a performer and charges Lori for his shows. Lori has a room she keeps her bowling trophies in.

Bab[ies] do not fit in stockpiled onesies. Call put out for twosies. Baby photos prove to be impossible due to incongruence of baby moods. Somebody is always screaming.

Grandmother (father's side, undocumented, hospital bed and pain medication. Has to remove the oxygen from the front of her face in order to speak):

I never liked the twins. Separate they were fine, but they were never separate. When I saw the ultrasound I wanted to tell her to get an abortion, I hinted to her that it was okay because no one can really say these things. No one expected them to live when they came out.

Everyone was smiling, but not because they were beautiful, they weren't beautiful. They took after their mother's side, all of them are two-faced anyway. I've got other grandchildren. At least they were able to wear the clothes I bought for them.

They take turns stacking blocks. Baby One knows letters A, C, E, G and baby two knows B, D, F, H. Together their voices make the sound, "Mama," and alone, if they could be alone, it's a repetitive, "Ma ma ma ma ma."

Deleted Scenes:

We did it out of curiosity more than anything else. Nobody knew what these bab[ies] would look like until we showed up at their house with a video camera. It was very normal really. They have older children too, and they were running around the house and the bab[ies] were screaming. It still wasn't guaranteed they were going to live yet. The doctors considered removing one of the heads, but then the other head would be left with a half paralyzed body. You know how when they remove a tree from the ground, there's still a stump sticking out? I bet it would've looked like that, just a stump of a head, like it never really grew at all. The remaining twin could've really said that they had lost a part of themselves. It would've made a good show. We could've titled it something like *My Parents Killed My Twin Sister Who Was Attached To Me*. What we had was probably better, but there were so many possibilities. That's what was exciting about it. The doctors were excited, we were excited. We were all excited together, but speaking different languages. They wanted the bab[ies] to live and we wanted television. Television that did what was best for the bab[ies], of course.

The IRS contacts the parents and says, "You have two children listed here, but only one body." The father sends a letter back and says, "Yes, but I have two mouths to feed." The IRS changes all of their forms to read: We count children by stomachs, not mouths.

The child[ren] are repeatedly brought in front of the school honor board for allegations of cheating. "Student One deliberately looked at Student Two's paper during every test and every homework assignment. It appears that Student One deliberately changed answers to appear different from Student Two." The Supreme Court issues a verdict that people conjoined by a minimum of two body parts cannot be discriminated against and such discrimination would be considered a hate crime.

Classmate (allegedly, sent to the principal, but denied accusations):

Two heads are better than one.

On the softball team they are counted as one player, because they need both their legs to run. The coach calls them by their last name only. They become the first people to hit a homerun simultaneously. The Guinness Book of World Records refuses to acknowledge their feat, claiming they are not playing by the rules.

When it is discovered they can drive together, two hands belonging to two separate brains, steering the car in the same direction, the government begins experimenting (undocumented, only evidenced in the YouTube video titled CONSPIRACY THEORY 25 now deleted) with cutting bodies in half and gluing them together to see if they'll make a whole. There's grainy footage of people with a line down the middle of their body whose faces don't quite add up, but it could have been done with marker.

Video Commentary (allegedly, sounds like the voice of a young person. He yells for most of the video, parts of his speech becoming incomprehensible at times): they could at least pick people who go well together. The eyes never matched up and the noses, they were all over the place. It was most interesting when they put an introvert and an extrovert together. The extrovert would be screaming and the introvert would be suffering their pain in silence. It was very painful of course. People said, or would've said if they had known about it, that no experiment had been so cruel since the infamous Henry Harlow who took all those monkeys away from their mothers. This is what the government is doing, our government. We ask them about it and they refuse to talk, only mentioning something about fracturing, whatever that means. When one half died, the other half would start to die immediately. Four halves of bodies, all died at the same time, coming loose at the seams.

An article is written that nobody reads titled, "Proof of the collective unconscious?" that includes a video of the child[ren] typing together. In pencil someone scrawls: It's not collective if they're the only ones.

Deleted Scenes:

Everyone was excited about the driving special. It had been so long since they were last on TV and the nation was desperate for an update. We got all these letters, the inaccuracy in them showed how badly we needed another show. A lot of them said things like, "What happened to that two-headed girl?" Doctors were even writing us. We had more access than they did. The parents kept insisting there was nothing wrong with their children. That's really what we wanted to show with that special, just how normal the children were. They did everything that normal sixteen-year olds do, except I don't know that they dated at all. No one was sure that they'd be able to drive, so we were all elated when it came naturally to them. We filmed them talking online with their friends. It was strange though, they never needed to discuss what they were going to say and referred to themselves as "I" rather than "we." I guess people are still "I," even if their "I" includes more than one person. It seemed sort of nice in a way, someone to keep you company all the time. I think that's how they got through it, they had the other person to support them whenever anything went wrong. The sort of thing people want from their spouses, but never really get because no matter how close you are with someone, they'll always be some distance away. Not so with these girls, they will never be any distance away.

In college, Student One is able to register for classes first and Student Two is stuck taking classes like "Basket Weaving" and "English Composition 102." They are charged tuition and a half, not minding that they are only counted as one and a half percent of themselves when there's money involved. They attend sorority recruitment, but the only sorority that accepts them has room for one more girl and not two. They live in a house with three other girls and they are the only ones forced to share a room.

When they graduate, they must order a robe made for an obese man, the neck still too small for both their heads. The announcer puts their names in the wrong order and when they protest, he says, "How was I supposed to know which one comes first?" One leg trips walking down the stairs, but the other one stays steady, holding both of them up.

Frat boy (undocumented, name changed):

We all talked about it, whether or not we'd fuck her. We had this one pledge, he's not in the frat anymore, but we made him go up to her at a bar and buy her a drink, I guess two drinks, one for each of the heads. He, uh, started flirting with them and stuff and they didn't seem to know what to do. They started giggling and acting all like the fat girls do when we flirt with them. I think they thought that he really liked them. Later he said that he felt bad for them, that they were actually really nice and that one of the heads was sort of cute and he was kind of wondering how many boobs they had. This is embarrassing, but we started making fun of him, saying shit like, "Two-head fucker" and stuff. One guy started talking about how they could give head to two people at the same time, I mean, they could give two people head at the same time. He wasn't wrong. Does it like, count as a threesome? To fuck a girl like that? There's only one vagina. Maybe that's a good thing. I wouldn't want to be inside a girl at the same time as someone else. That would be sort of gay.

They rent a two-bedroom, two-bathroom apartment on the nice side of town. They spend Monday, Wednesday, and Friday in one bedroom and Sunday, Tuesday, Thursday in the other. Saturdays they pass out drunk in the bathtub, double the drinks flowing through the same amount of blood veins. They build toilets facing each other so they can both throw up at the same time. When one twin shits, the other hand wipes up the mess.

Bartender:

They shared drinks, one cup, two straws. When I asked them why they didn't each get their own, they said, "I get drunk too fast," but man those girls could chug a cocktail. They liked sweet drinks, you know, fruity things. They could dance without looking at each other, their arms moving in unison. They even got low at the same time. They had really good balance, I guess because they're so wide. They didn't tip well though, I thought they'd have more money, from press and stuff. Isn't that how people like them make their money? When I took my smoke break, they were out there too. One girl would inhale the smoke in and the other would exhale out and they would switch. They got people to give them free cigarettes that way.

They go shopping at maternity stores to find clothes wide enough for their body. Nobody ever thinks they are pregnant. They can't decide on a dress, so they buy two and bring it to the tailor who cuts them in half and sews each half together. They wear it to their first interview where they print out two resumes that say the same thing.

Boss:

I needed to fulfill a diversity requirement. It was a two for one.

They have two desks, two computers, two staplers, two desk chairs, two cubicles, the mirror image of each other. They take twice as long as everyone else to do their work, dashing from cubicle to cubicle every few minutes. The real dilemma is when both phones ring at the same time and they are stuck pulling in opposite directions until the ringing ceases.

Coworker:

They get the mail of two people, even though they do the same job. Half of their letters are the same thing, only with a different name on it. People are so careful to be politically correct these days, but I'm just going to say it: they only have one body, two hands, they need each other to open the envelope, why make them do more work than they need to do for the sake of feelings?

Deleted Scenes:

It might have been a mistake to make the show a regular thing. Everyone wanted to see them do tricks. We got letters asking for us to film them on the toilet. People literally said things like, "Where does the shit come out?" as if they had no understanding of the human body. We kept seeing how far we could push it. We asked them to do some crazy things. So yes, I do feel partially responsible for what ultimately happened to them. But what was I supposed to do? I was under a lot of pressure from my superiors.

They each make an online dating account, using pictures that flatter their personal head. Under "About Me" they each write: "Autonomy is very important to me. I'm striving to be my own person every day and now I'm looking for someone to be independent with me." Under "The Deepest Secret You Are Willing To Reveal" they write: "My favorite movie is *Legally Blonde*. I know it's a stupid movie, but it's so fun to watch." Under "Size" they say: "More to love." When they say more, they mean more people, but they don't tell anyone that.

They have competitions to see who can get more men asking them to take their shirts off or women asking if they'd be willing to turn gay. They delete the messages that say: "Why does it look like someone is next to you all the time?" They talk to the same men and set up different dates at different times and the men are always surprised when they both show up.

Restaurant bill (found on floor of restaurant, swept up and thrown in garbage):

> 1 glass beer
>
> 4 glass wine
>
> 1 calamari
>
> 1 lasagna
>
> 1 spaghetti marinara
>
> 1 ice cream sundae

Waiter (allegedly):

The three of them came together, but it was clear that one of them was only there for support in that her head was being supported by their shared body. The hostess didn't know how to seat them and so she led them to a round table and let them seat themselves. The man kept putting his hands on the one girl's face and the other one was just hanging there. She wasn't the third wheel as much as she was the second head. I kept refilling her water glass, but she didn't order anything and the other two didn't offer. The girl on the date just kept drinking wine and after awhile she started slurring her words. I bet the other one would've too, if she had talked at all, but she didn't say a word the whole time. They ordered dessert and I asked them if they wanted three spoons and they said they only wanted two. They didn't even finish their dessert. The man paid. He wasn't very attractive, but I guess you have to be a special type to go out with a girl like that.

Police report:

Subject 1 and Subject 2 appeared intoxicated. They were having both a verbal and physical altercation. Neither Subject was harmed during the altercation, as they were unable to make contact with the other's face. Allegedly, Subject 1 had sexual relations with a man without the consent of Subject 2. Subject 2 reports screaming repeatedly, "No, no, no, I don't want you to do this, stop, this is my body too, you have no right to do this." I asked Subject 2 if they wanted to file charges and they said yes, but Subject 1 refused, saying she had a right to use her body however she wanted. Since we were unable to separate the girls, we put them in the back of the squad car and brought them to precinct, where they are in the holding cell until they calm down. Unsure how to proceed from here.

They complain when they are only given one set of handcuffs, only take one mug shot, and given one phone call even though they call the same person and say the same thing when they are finally rewarded with two. They find separate jobs and separate apartments, sharing custody of their single body.

Deleted scenes:

I mean, yes, it was regrettable what happened to their lives after that show, but we tried our hardest to respect their wishes. It was their idea to have the show on two different days with two different titles. It wasn't our fault that we had the same footage for both the girls, we weren't trying to imply that they were the same person, but they did all the same things. They weren't talking to each other at the time, it was a series of interactions with other people and mishaps trying to do things with one hand or one foot. They kept eating foods that required both a fork and a knife, we weren't trying to ridicule them, who orders a steak when they only have one hand at their disposal? It made the trials difficult too, neither one of them could ever meet with their lawyer in private and eventually all the lawyers just quit. I wouldn't say it's our fault, no, I think it's just one of the challenges people want to know about. It did make good TV though, when neither of the girls could agree on what to wear and they just started going shirtless all over the place and you could really see their body, breasts so far apart, skin melded together. It didn't look natural, but that was the point.

They continue their fight until they receive a pile of letters from men who only love two-headed women and they are the only ones that can fulfill their desires. They start working part time at a strip club, with their own special room in the back. There is a Cerberus painted on the door, even though the dog has three heads instead of two. A warning above: What you are about to see is very sensual. Everyone is careful never to use the word "freak."

Nurse:

They showed up at the hospital with blood on their hands. We couldn't separate them, not that they could ever be separated, but when we were finally able to pull their fingers apart—a death grip, that's what it's called—we found the fetus inside. They were wailing in unison, it was eerie. The sobs coming out of their throats at the same time. The interesting thing was that the baby was almost fully developed, but it had no head. Otherwise it was perfect, it was just missing the most important part. That wasn't the last time we saw them like that. It was almost like they had built it into their routine the way normal people go to the gym. The miscarriages kept coming, one after another. All of the babies were missing something. Even between the two of them, they couldn't make one whole baby. The doctors didn't know what was wrong, the uterus was healthy. Those poor girl[s]. I don't know how we would even fill out a birth certificate for them if any baby were to live.

Deleted Scenes:

It wasn't like their fame stopped after the show was over. Everyone wanted to know what they were doing. Fans said, "We want to know what is happening behind the scenes." They wanted to see what was happening when we weren't filming. They told us what was on TV was too normal. They said that no girl with two heads could act normal like that.

Pictures of the twins start appearing in tabloids. THE TWINS AND PRINCE HARRY??? Pictures of them with white powder, bongs in the background. TWINS BREAK UP BRAD AND ANGELINA, EXCLUSIVE INSIDE. TWINS BEACH BODY, HOW TO GET THIS IN SHAPE. They shoot a *Cosmo* cover while wearing an animal print dress especially designed for them. BIGGEST TURN ON: A GUY WHO CAN LOVE BOTH OF THEIR FACES, GET THE SCOOP INSIDE. TWINS FACING FORECLOSURE??? HOW THEY SQUANDERED THEIR TELEVISION FORTUNE. They hide their faces when they walk outdoors so the paparazzi cannot snap any pictures.

Doctor (name undisclosed):

It was shocking, really. They were so healthy for so long and no one could explain why. They had the perfect amount of organs for their body. Anymore or any less and they could've died. That was one thing they were really good about, reaching out to families who had lost conjoined twins, because most conjoined twins do die, either they are stillborn or cannot survive for very long outside of the womb. When one of their brains had a stroke though, the other side couldn't take it. She held on for as long as she could, it was actually a period of several weeks, dragging her dead sister around. She kept saying that she felt lonely and that it smelled. She had never been alone before and we got her several psychiatrists to evaluate her state and put her on anti-depressants, but it didn't seem to do anything and eventually the body just shut down. Imagine not being able to function without another person like that. That is complete dependence, both physically and mentally.

Recorded examples of separation:

Angelica and Angelina: They were connected at the chest and abdomen. Hearts beating against the same walls. Doctor: "The only physical reminder of their ordeal will be a long scar from the chest to the belly button."

Hassan and Hussein: Their hands were not connected, but they held each other anyway. The caption on the picture: they are still conjoined, even though they have been cut apart.

Maria Paz and Maria Jose: Maria Jose died three days after the surgery because Maria Paz took all of the organs.

Rital and Ritag: Ritag was pumping all the blood for Rital and she was too young to say that it was out of love as her heart started failing and they cut them apart.

Clarence and Carl: They were separated one day at a time, balloons expanding their skin. They wear helmets, in the absence of each other.

Lakshmi: Some say that she was the goddess of wealth with four arms and four legs and others say she was born with a parasitic twin that her parents were too poor to get removed. Her mother said that before she was born she had a dream that she was to build a temple to the goddess Lakshmi and did so inside herself, using her own cells to build the body. Lakshmi could only sit in the puddle of her limbs, her other-self born with club feet and useless hands. When she was two years old, all the excesses of herself were removed and she learned to walk on her own, using only braces to hold her legs together.

Elliot and His Demonic Daughters

Elliot always wanted a large family. He'd had two siblings growing up and to some people this would be considered large but was not the type of large that Elliot wanted. Elliot wanted a family so large that it would be spilling out of the large home that Elliot had also always wanted.

Elliot set about collecting children. Before he started collecting children, Elliot had collected a wife and a career with a promising future because Elliot was a promising businessman. Elliot first met his wife at a bar. He hadn't expected to meet his wife at a bar as Elliot didn't respect the kind of women that drank a lot. Elliot's future wife was not drinking a lot. She was the "DD" for the night and even though Elliot knew that "DD" stood for "Designated Driver," he still called her "DeeDee" as a pet name. His wife's actual name was Janine.

When Elliot first met DeeDee she was leaning over her friend who was sitting on the ground and vomiting all over herself. Before he had even talked to her, Elliot could picture DeeDee as the mother of his children, as children often sat on the floor and vomited on themselves as well. Elliot helped DeeDee walk her friend to the car and asked her to go on a date with him. They were married several months later.

DeeDee used to be a dental hygienist, but after they got married she became a stay-at-home mother. This was fine with DeeDee. There was nothing she liked more than staying home and mothering. She popped out their first child, a boy, with no problems. A week after their son was born, Elliot purchased a gun. He would do anything to protect his child.

There were complications with the second pregnancy. DeeDee was bedridden for weeks and then the baby got stuck in her tubes and they had to cut her open to get it out. The doctors said it would be extremely risky for DeeDee to become pregnant again and DeeDee and Elliot cried and cried over their unborn children and DeeDee became quite depressed for several months, which was later diagnosed as post-partum depression.

Because DeeDee and Elliot were unable to have any more biological children, they started researching the adoption process. They were good candidates for adoption because they had a nice house and a steady income and DeeDee was able to stay home with the children. Initially Elliot wanted to adopt another tiny baby. He loved their little fingers and little toes and the way they smelled and gurgled and smiled and said "dada" and "daddy" like it was an accomplishment. DeeDee, the motherly figure that she was, suggested that maybe they should adopt children that were older, siblings perhaps, children that no one wanted. How could a person say no to such an offer?

The wait for a tiny baby was years and years long and required a great deal of money. The wait for older children was quite short and actually came with a small monthly stipend for each child, which was a pleasant surprise for Elliot who didn't actually need the money, but appreciated it nonetheless.

DeeDee and Elliot adopted three sisters. It was believed that the three sisters had experienced some level of trauma in their previous housing situation before they had been removed, though it was unknown as to exactly how much. The adoption counselor warned DeeDee and Elliot that the girls had "a lot of needs" and suggested that perhaps DeeDee and Elliot did not have the experience needed to take care of such children. The more the counselor insisted that Elliot was incapable of caring for the children, the more Elliot wanted them. He envisioned their transformation, the way they would become model daughters in his household.

DeeDee decorated the third bedroom in their home in pink. She bought flowered bedspreads and a matching wallpaper border. She couldn't imagine a nicer bedroom for little girls. DeeDee, Elliot, and their two biological children travelled together to the adoption agency to pick them up. Their biological children were still too young to understand what was happening despite Elliot repeatedly telling them that they were going to get new siblings.

Elliot could tell that DeeDee didn't like the way that the girls were dressed at the adoption agency. Their clothes were too big and too small and too ripped and had cheesy slogans in the front like "Angel." If the girls had been anyone else's children besides theirs, Elliot knew that DeeDee would have muttered "trashy" underneath her breath. Because they were her children, DeeDee reached her arms out for a hug. The girls did not oblige.

"There will be a transitional period," the adoption counselor had said. This was what Elliot reminded DeeDee that first night when she cried over how little the girls loved her. "They just met you," Elliot said. "Give them some time." DeeDee wept some more and said "But I already love them." DeeDee did already love three little girls. They were the conceptual little girls that she had made up in her head that loved braiding hair and painting pictures.

The three actual girls that lived in their house liked cutting the hair off dolls and threatening to kill one another in various ways. "They really are quite creative," Elliot said. Though they were still small, the girls knew a variety of swearwords, including some that DeeDee had never heard before. Elliot and DeeDee decided that it would be better if they moved the girls to separate rooms. It was then that Elliot and DeeDee learned that the girls were possessed by the devil or perhaps various devils.

Elliot didn't believe in the devil any more than any other ordinary person believed in the devil. He had a church that he attended regularly with DeeDee and the children and had watched several movies about possession, though he couldn't claim that he was a fan of the horror genre. Perhaps if he had seen more movies he would have been faster to realize how deeply and irrevocably his adopted children were possessed by Satan.

Elliot and DeeDee moved their small biological children into the master bedroom with them temporarily in order to give each of the three girls their own room. They figured if the girls were separated, they would cause fewer problems. The first night the girls were separated they screamed the whole night long, causing DeeDee and

Elliot's biological children to wake and scream along with them. Elliot, a businessman, needed his sleep and could not have five screaming children in his household. He invested in some gags that would keep the girls silent while they slept. "Go to sleep," he said, as he loving put the gags in their mouths.

The second night the girls banged on the walls with their fists. Elliot did not know that the fists of little girls could make so much noise. Later he realized that's because demons were possessing their fists and demon fists are quite loud. DeeDee reported that in the morning their precious biological children were imitating the noises by banging their hands on the floor. After work, Elliot stopped by the hardware store and picked up some rope. Before the girls went to sleep that night, he tied their wrists behind their backs. "This is for your own good," he said. "You need to learn to stay still."

When Elliot woke in the morning for work, the girls were still bound and gagged, but the walls of their rooms were covered in blood red symbols. That was the first moment it occurred to him that the devil might be living inside their small souls.

Elliot wasn't Catholic, but based off his knowledge of movies, Catholics were the most knowledgeable about demonic possession. Instead of eating lunch during his lunch hour, Elliot sought out a Catholic priest at the nearby Catholic Church. Unlike the movies, the Catholic priest was quite skeptical that the girls were possessed. "Have you taken them to see a psychologist?" he asked Elliot. Elliot explained to the priest that he was a rational man, a businessman, not the type of person to believe in a possession that was not a possession. If he, of all people, believed that there was a demon inside of his children, then certainly there was a demon inside of them.

The Catholic priest agreed to come to DeeDee and Elliot's home the following evening to witness the so-called "demonic activity" that Elliot had described. Elliot hired a security service to install cameras throughout the house. He knew from movies that demons liked cameras more than anything else, which was amazing to think about because when the demons were born at the beginning of time cameras hadn't even existed yet.

When the priest arrived at their home, DeeDee had let the girls out of their graffitied rooms for some structured playtime and the girls were contorting their limbs in various unnatural positions. "They say they're doing gymnastics," DeeDee whispered. The smaller biological children were standing off to the side attempting to imitate the demonic children, though of course, they were too young, too small, too free of demons to move their bodies in such ways. "Little girls are flexible creatures," the priest said.

DeeDee made her famous tater-tot casserole for dinner, which the priest thoroughly enjoyed and the demon girls threw at each other across the table. "Girls, stop playing with your food," Elliot said. It was then that the oldest adopted child threw a handful of casserole at his face and proceeded to wipe the rest of her food all over her clothes. Elliot had no choice but to send her to her room. Unlike the previous evenings Elliot didn't restrain her in any way. He ordered her to put on her pajamas and brush her teeth, which she did after only an ordinary amount of convincing. No child, not even ones with wholly human souls, liked to get ready for bed.

The other children were allowed to stay up until bedtime and watch an approved animated film about a princess and a dragon. Based off the girls' behavior when the TV was on, Elliot had ascertained that demons also liked television, though he couldn't blame them for that one, as Elliot himself often indulged in a good movie or show.

After putting all of their children to bed, the priest, DeeDee, and Elliot lined up on the couch to watch the demonic footage. Elliot was disappointed for the first several hours when the girls mainly slept like they really were girls and not demons at all. DeeDee and the priest engaged in a board game while they waited. Elliot just stared at the screen. The devil, he expected, was an intelligent sort of creature. He wouldn't reveal himself immediately. It would take patience, perseverance, qualities that Elliot considered to be godly.

DeeDee and the priest were on the third board game when the clock struck midnight. The clock didn't really strike midnight as there were no striking clocks in their suburban home. Instead the fingers of their wall clocks and the digits on their cell phones turned to twelve-zero. That's when the girls started to move. They got up simultaneously, as though their bodies were connected by strings. Elliot ushered DeeDee and the priest over to the television. He didn't want to make noise and let the girls know that they were watching, though certainly the demons knew that they were watching because the demons knew everything.

They started dancing. There was no music in the house. The girls were dancing to an internal demonic beat. Elliot was familiar with dancing. Back in college he had been to a variety of parties and clubs. He had seen women in their tiniest dresses, doing their dirtiest dances.

For his bachelor's party he even went to a strip club, though he hadn't had a very good time. The strippers all had a lot of cellulite and while he was certain that some of them were mothers, none of them had the motherly aesthetic that he preferred. He had questioned the morality of these various dirty dances, but he had never before suspected that a dance had been composed by the devil until he saw the movement of his adopted daughters. Their bodies were still undeveloped, still small and bony and yet when they danced, hips appeared. Their upper bodies shook as though they were having a seizure. The priest became so concerned that they were having some sort of epileptic fit that he suggested he go into their rooms and help them. Elliot reassured him that no, it wasn't a medical emergency, it was simply the devil.

The dancing stopped and Elliot was worried that the girls would simply return to bed and fall asleep and nothing would come of the priest's investigation. It was the same type of worry he felt when bringing his car to the auto mechanic only to discover that his car had begun to function normally on the ride there. Luckily for Elliot, the devil didn't let him down the way that his car did. The two younger girls sat on the edges of their beds and stared up at the cameras. They had never held Elliot's gaze in person, always looking away or down at the floor. On film, they seemed eager for eye contact, eager to connect with the people who were watching them from the living room. The oldest girl reached underneath her mattress. The resolution of the cameras was not good enough for Elliot to gauge just what it was that she was retrieving, though he knew from the look she gave the camera after she fetched whatever it was that it was something bad. He was not surprised when seconds later blood started streaming from both of her wrists and down to the floor. He wanted to stay and watch, see what her plan was next, but the priest insisted that they go into her room and stop her. She needed to be in a hospital, the priest said. DeeDee agreed, certainly the child's safety was more important than verifying the almost-guaranteed possession.

Elliot and the priest drove the girl to the hospital while DeeDee stayed home with the other children. In the emergency room, a doctor gave her a psychological evaluation. "She's sick," the priest told the doctor. "She's possessed," Elliot said. When Elliot said possessed, the doctor thought that he meant something else, meant that she was depressed or was wrangling with internal demons. He did not think that Elliot meant a literal demon, a creature that had forced itself into Elliot's adopted daughter's insides. The hospital agreed that it would be best for the girl to check in for an extended visit. They would put her on medication and give her counseling. Elliot knew those things would never work. Elliot knew the only thing that would work was exorcism. Elliot was certain that the priest, now thoroughly shook by the encounter, would be on his side and willing to perform the ritual.

"We don't really do exorcisms anymore," the priest said when Elliot asked. "You've watched too many movies. Your girls have legitimate troubles, but you will have to look for help in the human realm." Elliot, a promising businessman, was shocked by this response. Surely no rational man would think that his daughters were not possessed by demons. Wasn't the whole point of the church to help people that were in need? Who was more in need than Elliot and his demonic daughters?

When Elliot returned home, his two biological children were sitting on the floor in a pile of markers. The markers alone were egregious enough, his children so small and messy that they were primarily allowed the use of crayons, which caused far fewer stains in Elliot and DeeDee's large house. Worse, the children had no paper, but were using their arms as the canvas, drawing colored lines up and down their wrists just as the adopted daughter had the night before with a razor blade. Elliot was overcome with a rage of the type that he had never been overcome with before and Elliot was a man that rage often overcame. In high school, his girlfriend, a girl that he thought was the love of his life, left him for the captain of the swim team. The day of the break up, Elliot threatened to kill the captain of the swim team, kill himself, and at the moment of ultimate panic, kill the girl he thought was the love of his life. Because Elliot was at times a rational person, he did not kill anyone at all, but proceeded to get very drunk and throw up all over his garage.

There had been many times in his life when Elliot said kill and did not mean kill. "I could kill him," Elliot said to drivers that cut him off, to people who were rude in stressful situations. He had never killed anyone in those situations, merely uttered under his breath, left bad tips and passive-aggressive notes on cars. When he said, "I could kill them," about his adopted daughters, Elliot meant it. DeeDee found Elliot in the master bedroom sitting on the side of the bed and cradling the gun he had purchased when their son was born. "Oh Elliot," DeeDee said and put her arms around his shoulders and he cried into her stomach, a stomach that was enough months post-pregnancy that it had shrunken back to its normal size. "There are other things we can do," DeeDee said. It was her mother-voice, the one that she used on the children, the one she had been using on the drunk girl in the street the night that Elliot had met her. The voice infuriated Elliot and then calmed him, the way his own mother's voice did. Elliot put the gun down. He was not the sort of man who killed his own adopted children.

It was DeeDee's idea to try to get some monetary gain from the situation. If nothing else, they deserved reparations for their pain. Reparations, of course, in addition to the monthly check that they were cut for caring for the girls. They were honest in their intentions, the way that they had been honest when selling an old rocking chair that was on the verge of breaking. "Broken rocking chair," their internet advertisement had said. Someone had bought the rocking chair almost immediately. It didn't seem so strange then, that they would sell their demonic adopted children. "Demonic children," the advertisement read. DeeDee and Elliot explained all the behaviors their adopted girls had exhibited. "Oldest child still hospitalized," the post explained. Elliot, a promising businessman, knew that it was important to be honest when conducting those sorts of transactions.

They received many offers for the girls. It turned out that demonic daughters were even more valuable than broken rocking chairs. DeeDee and Elliot took the offer from the highest bidder who came to get the girls in his pickup truck. Elliot and DeeDee waved the girls off as they drove away. That night they went out to dinner with their biological children to celebrate and Elliot and DeeDee had sex for the first time in a long time even though DeeDee's body was incapable of having more children. "It's okay if we have a smaller family," Elliot said to DeeDee. "I still want to be with you even if we only ever have two children." DeeDee, who was much less stressed when the girls were gone, started sewing a series of quilts. Elliot's grandmother had been a wonderful quilter and he was pleased that DeeDee had taken up the project.

Sometime later there was a newspaper article about the man who had purchased the adopted daughters that said he had been charged with several cases of sexual assault on a child. Elliot recognized the picture of the man with his cleanly-shaved face and kind blue eyes. According to the article, he had used these kind blue eyes to lure children into his basement where he molested them. Elliot reviled pedophiles. He had not suspected that this man was a pedophile when he came to pick up the girls and Elliot believed that he had a fairly good radar for picking pedophiles out of a crowd. Usually, he thought, they had beards.

There was no mention of the girls in the article, no quotes about a demon in the household. As he was reading, Elliot got a tingling sensation on his back, the one that could mean a harmless itch or signify the presence of someone else in the room. He looked behind him. No one was there. It was one thing to believe that his adopted daughters had been possessed by demons and it was quite another to believe in an invisible presence in the room. He was safe, he assured himself. Still, he got up and walked around his office. He checked in the storage closet for monsters. He sprinkled some water on his face looking for something holy.

Clowns

When the ominous clowns started appearing, Harry had already been a clown for quite some time. His father had signed him up for clowning lessons when he was a small child, which was a joke in itself as Harry had always been tremendously unfunny. "It'll be fun, bud," his father said. He always called Harry "bud" instead of by his name and Harry had taken to the moniker, adopting it as his clown name. In some ways, Harry felt as though he would've been a clown regardless of his father signing him up for lessons. Some people were just born that way.

Harry was a sad clown because no one wanted to laugh at his joy. He painted his white face white and a big red frown around his lips. He wore a wig that was bald on top with strands of straw red hair around the bottom. A pair of overalls with a beach ball belly stuffed inside and a pair of oversized shoes that he tripped in when he wasn't even meaning to. He went to birthday parties where kids screamed and ran away. He went to clown gatherings where everyone brought a pie and spent the rest of the day cleaning whipped cream off their faces. He went on dates with girls from the internet who showed up and said,

"Oh, I didn't know that you dressed like a clown all the time." This was where he got his biggest laughs: the noises that girls made before they abandoned him at the bar alone.

The ominous clowns started appearing in October. Clowns with sharp teeth, swinging by themselves on playgrounds. Clowns lurked in cul-de-sacs with chainsaws and axes, ready to chop off the faces of children. They were rogue clowns, the type that didn't pay their dues in the clown union. Elementary schools shut down for the day at the threat of clowns. Harry knew that such threats were more than making children laugh too hard. These were killer clowns, clowns that were determined to ruin the name of clowning for everyone.

He used his best white paint and his squeakiest nose when he went clown hunting. He put the tiny handgun he purchased inside of his giant pants. Having things that were comically-different sizes was a classic clown trick. He put a baseball bat and a flashlight in the passenger seat of his fire-truck-red Smart Car and a whole box of whipped-cream-based pies. Like his clown friends always said: there was more than one way to take down a clown gone rogue.

Clowns, all of them, like to hang out where children play. The evil clowns were no exception to the rule. News reports made it seem like they were everywhere, covering parks and playgrounds like grains of sand. On his first night, Harry struck out. He found a homeless man in one of the parks and a crying teenage girl in another, but no one with giant red lips like a scar. Perhaps, he thought, the news had been hyperbolic, as the news had a tendency to be. To watch television was to believe that people were constantly and always dying when for the most part, people continued to live long and tedious lives.

On his second night out, Harry found a big red shoe that had fallen off the foot of an errant clown. On his third, he found a squeaky nose. If only, he lamented, the evil clowns could have a downloadable schedule on their website like their more legitimate brethren. When he finally spotted them, it was like seeing a dog pretending to be a dinosaur. Such poorly-applied makeup, no skill put into their fake fangs and sunken eyes. Harry wasn't even sure that their weapons were real. He watched them from behind a bush, plotting his plan of action. Clowns always had a plan no matter how clumsy they seemed when they were performing.

He was about to move forward with his plan of attack when he felt a stinging in his buttocks. Audiences found butts to be quite funny, especially if it involved some sort of excrement leaving the butt or a pain in the butt. Harry didn't find it funny when his butt was lit up, electrified with the stings of a Taser. He had never been one of those clowns whose gimmick was the faking of extreme violence.

"Got 'em!" a voice said. A police officer, a real one, not a clown pretending to be the law. One of the few professions where they took their uniform as seriously as the clowns took theirs. They put handcuffs on Harry and said, "We've been trying to catch you for a while, mister." Harry tried to protest, tried to explain that no, despite the baseball bat and the handgun and the oversized shoes and nose, he was a good clown who was trying to catch the bad clowns. "Sure you are," the police officers said and laughed. Harry, always making people laugh at his sorrows.

The officers let Harry make his phone call before booking him in the county jail. He called one of his clown friends, Damon, who showed up in a tiny car packed to the brim with other clowns. They jumped out of the car, tripping over one another as they went. "We better arrest these guys too," the officers said. "The cell is really full of clowns tonight." The officer paused a moment and said, "The cell is full of clowns every night," and then laughed and laughed at his own joke until one of the clowns, pie in hand, hit him in the face.

The rest of the clowns rushed in. They attacked the cell door with oversized plastic hammers. They squirted liquid out of fake flowers attached to their chests into the faces of the police, and as the officers screamed and cried, Harry realized that they must have replaced their water with pepper spray. It would be funny, he thought, if it wasn't happening to me. Another officer tried to rush the scene only to slip on a banana peel. An alarm sounded as the plastic hammers broke through the steel door and they, the good clowns, the benevolent ones, squeezed themselves like sausages into the tiny car and off into the night.

Carnival Surprise

People often mistook Josh for a Walmart greeter because of the smiley-face pin he wore on his chest each day. He had never worked at Walmart, though he did do a brief stint at Kmart the summer before he had started graduate school. It was just that he really liked smiley faces. They made him feel smiley on the inside.

Josh was a man filled with passion. Some people never find what they want to do in life and Josh was lucky. Josh knew as soon as he joined the Student Life Committee his sophomore year of college. Above all else, Josh wanted to curate events for college students.

There are many amazing things about the world and one of those amazing things is that there is an advanced degree for people who want to spend their lives curating events for college students called "Student Affairs and Higher Education."

Josh graduated at a time of cuts in the academic community. No one wanted to hire someone to spend more money to distract the students from their studying. That's when it all started, when Josh decided to throw a small birthday carnival for his friend Heather.

Josh had been in love with Heather for all of college. People often asked if they were dating, which hurt his heart a little each time they said it. "No," he said. "Just friends," and everyone laughed because there was something funny about unrequited love.

While Josh was getting his master's degree, Heather had become a high-powered lawyer who wore suits each day. Josh never wore a suit. Josh always wore jeans, a T-shirt, and his smiley-face pin.

Josh wanted to do something really nice for Heather's birthday and he knew how much she had enjoyed the spring carnival the college had thrown each year and so he took out a small loan and rented some equipment and set up a carnival in Heather's front yard for her to wake up to in the morning.

Heather was very shocked and surprised and said, "Oh my gosh, Josh," and then they laughed because "gosh" and "Josh" rhymed. Heather rode the rides a couple of times and ate a plate of cheese curds and grabbed some cotton candy and then said, "Well, I have to go to work, thanks again, Josh." She hugged him and it felt so nice.

Josh still had the rides and the food stands rented for the rest of the day so he checked Facebook, one of his favorite social networks, to see who else was having a birthday that day. Josh had an extensive Facebook presence due to his heavy involvement in various collegiate activities. He felt it was important to send friend requests to as many students as possible in order to keep them fully informed about all of the events happening on campus. He was pleased when he found that Byron, another friend from college, also had a birthday that day.

Josh and Byron had never been particularly close and had not kept in touch after college, but Josh was able to find Byron's address through the alumni directory that he kept in his car at all times. He led the carnival on a procession through the suburbs of Chicago before arriving at Byron's house. Byron was even more ecstatic than Heather had been. Byron apparently, had not yet gotten a job since graduating three years prior and was still living in his parents' house. He had gained forty pounds and his girlfriend had left him. The carnival was the only nice thing anyone had done for him in years.

"Thanks, man," he said as tears rolled down his cheeks.

Josh had such a nice time setting up carnivals that day that he extended his rental contracts and brought his traveling student activity center from birthday to birthday. Soon he was getting requests from former classmates, ones that he hadn't even really known, to show up at their doors. This is when he started getting behind. Many people had relocated after college and sometimes it took him several days to reach their homes. Still, he vowed, he was going to get a carnival to everyone who wanted one.

Instead of a birthday carnival, it became known as the carnival surprise. Graduates of the college woke up on random days throughout the year to find Josh standing at their door with his smiley-face pin and a myriad of rides behind him.

"I was worried you weren't going to make it," they said before they hugged him. It was always that hug that brought Josh the most satisfaction.

Some of Josh's former classmates, ones who had been less successful, started to join on Josh's caravan. They traveled from Chicago to San Francisco, to Texas, to Boston, to Canada. The only Student Affairs counselor to ever bring the activities to the alumni in their homes. There were only a couple of people who didn't appreciate the surprise, who said, "Who are you? Please leave my property." Everyone else was so happy to have a party, so happy to see his smiling face and his smiley face and to shove cotton candy down their throats early in the morning.

Mr. Skull

She was nothing like they thought she would be when they went to visit her in Russia. It was to be expected, of course. She was in Russia, had lived there for the entirety of her unclaimed existence. But the pictures of her hadn't suggested that she would be anything like she was.

They had two children already. They weren't trying to solve anything. He was a math teacher and after school a football coach for the junior varsity team. If he knew how to do anything it was find solutions and tackle problems.

His name was Mr. Skull. Maybe that's why he decided to adopt a special-needs child from Russia. A skeletal head left to its own devices would never adopt a child from Russia.

Several months previous, a member of the senior varsity football team, a sophomore, a real gifted guy, the kind who would've gotten a full ride to a D1 school and maybe even gone pro, was charged with the raping of two women. On both occasions, he had allegedly broken into the homes of the women he violated late at night. Mr. Skull didn't want to say that it was worse that he had broken into the homes and had not simply committed the acts on the streets, but there was a level of deliberation included in a break-in that made him feel uncomfortable.

He and his wife, Mrs. Skull, had been talking about adoption before the arrest. She worked for a nonprofit. She had come to all his D3 football games in college and that was important to him. If someone can sit and watch a D3 football game they can do almost anything.

The most egregious allegation that came out during the arrest of the football player was that one of the violations had occurred in front of the victim's four-year-old son. Mr. Skull imagined the child standing there, wearing the same rocket ship pajama bottoms he himself had worn as a child. Mr. Skull had never witnessed a rape or been violated in any way. He'd had a good childhood and had gotten good grades and been involved in many after-school activities including year-round sports and math team. He didn't know why he thought of his rocket ship pajamas at that particular moment.

Mr. Skull had started balding at a young age and since then had been shaving the remains of his hair. The best party joke that ever existed was his head. His wife was blonde. She had put on some weight since they had gotten married. That was normal. So had he. Muscle doesn't really turn to fat. The body is not capable of magic, but it seemed this way. He couldn't lift the things he used to. He couldn't pummel man after man to the ground.

His favorite feature of his wife were her toenails. They were small and neatly trimmed like pearls of the feet. He was not above sucking on them, cherishing the delicacy of her bones. Mr. Skull's own toenails were filled with fungus, his toes broken and crooked from years of football.

There were rumors that the senior varsity coaches had known about the rapes. That the boy had bragged about these occasions in the locker room. According to the rumors, the coaches had not reported him to the police because "boys said all sorts of things in the locker room" and because "they were having a great football season." Mr. Skull hadn't known about the rape, but after the boy was charged he began hearing rumors about the kid showing off his dick in the back of various classrooms. It was too much for a child to both be gifted at football and have a big penis.

Mr. Skull had been popular in high school. Everyone called him "Skull." Mr. Skull was popular as a teacher too. He was well liked amongst his fellow teachers and his students gave him good evaluations. He was offered the position of teaching the gifted students but he declined, saying that he would rather teach those in need. Math made sense to him in a way that other things didn't make sense to him. He wanted to teach people about numbers.

They had received pictures of the child up for adoption. She had some special needs. They examined the background of the pictures, carefully looking for any sign of abuse or neglect. It wasn't that they wouldn't take an abused child, not that at all, but they wanted to know what they were getting themselves into. They were pleased when her surroundings were clean. They commented on how she wasn't smiling in any of the pictures, but maybe it was a cultural thing. They didn't know very much about Russia. They told themselves they would go for an exploratory visit. They would try not to get too attached to anything. But Mrs. Skull had already hung the pictures of the child on the refrigerator next to crude drawings done by the biological Skull children.

On the airplane to Russia, Mr. Skull and his family were served a warmed chicken breast with a variety of vegetables on the side and a small roll with a little tray of butter. Mr. Skull's son, Thomas Skull, declared that he liked airplane food and didn't know why people complained about it so much. Tommy Skull had been born after they stopped serving food on domestic flights. He did not remember 9/11. He had blonde hair and blue eyes and wore a neon green soccer shirt with the word "SKULL" written on the back.

Emma Skull, the littlest of the Skulls, dropped her roll on the floor and cried until Mr. Skull handed over his roll to her even though he had wanted to eat it. It was important to make sacrifices for one's children.

If nothing else, they told each other, it would be a cultural experience for the children. It was important for their children to be cultured. Mr. Skull didn't speak Russian, but had purchased a dictionary of Russian words. He studied words like "привет" and "пожалуйста" and "спасибо." Mr. Skull liked that the letters looked like symbols. Symbols were a thing that he understood until he tried to make them come out of his mouth and then he fumbled over his tongue and resorted to speaking English.

Halfway through their first day in Russia, Thomas Skull told Mr. Skull that his favorite part of the country was how they also had McDonald's "just like back home," though he expressed that he would like it better if the menus were in English.

"Chicken McNuggets, the universal language," Mr. Skull joked though he knew that math was the real universal language.

Later that night in the hotel room, Mrs. Skull confessed to Mr. Skull that she "desperately needed this child." It was what she'd always wanted that she never knew she'd always wanted. Mr. Skull liked how she smelled the same way in Russia that she did in the United States. He liked the familiarity of her body.

When they arrived at the orphanage (it wasn't called that, an orphanage, but that's what he called it in his head), they didn't want to show them the girl. "Why are you hiding my child from me?" Mr. Skull asked because he already knew it was destiny.

When someone was threatening one of his children Mr. Skull got the same feeling he got on the football field when he was trying to tackle someone with the ball. He wanted to pummel them into the ground so hard that they could never touch his baby again. Babies were what he called women, children, and footballs.

The women, who were really harmless after all, not worthy of pummeling to the ground, took the Skull family to a small backroom. It reminded Mr. Skull of picking out a kitten at the Humane Society as a small child. He selected the kitten he wanted to play with from the wire cage, a small orange tabby cat that would later become a large orange tabby cat with an abnormally needy disposition and they had sat in a windowless white room covered in cat fur and half-destroyed toys while Mr. Skull, then Boy-Skull, tried to bond with this kitten and decide if it was going to be his forever. The kitten wouldn't engage. He walked around the room, swatting at the fake mice and rolling on the floor and ignoring the Skulls who sat staring at him, wondering aloud,

"Is he ours? Should we take him home?" But Boy-Skull had already decided that this cat was his, he'd brought him into this room and that sealed their fate. He felt the same way, years later, sitting on the floor of the veterinarian's office, trying to stick his cat's tongue back into its mouth from where it was hanging grotesquely after receiving medicine to put it to sleep and out of its cancerous, diabetic misery. He did not see why a child should be any different than a cat.

The women walked the child into the room and sat her on a chair. They mumbled to each other in Russian, words that Mr. Skull didn't understand. He felt as though they were purposefully obscuring their speech. He wanted to tell them, "Speak more clearly," as if he would somehow find something recognizable in those syllables. As a math teacher, Mr. Skull knew a lot about using language that people did not understand.

They had thought she wasn't photogenic. "Maybe it's the light making her face look that way," they said. "Maybe the cameras they use in Russia aren't as good as our cameras," they said. In actuality, it was just that she wasn't very good looking. She wore the same frown that she had in the photograph. A grim line across the face. Her head was more of a square shape than an oval. As a math teacher, Mr. Skull knew a lot about shapes.

It wasn't as though he thought she would break into a smile upon meeting them, say, "My family!" She couldn't say that because she didn't speak English. Instead he had thought that she would break into a smile and say, "Моя семья," which was the translation of "my family" in Russian that Mr. Skull had looked up on the internet.

Before every football game, Mr. Skull liked to envision the win. How he would pump his arms into the air, let out a guttural noise that at any other time would be embarrassing but in football was an acceptable breach of decorum. After a win, he always said, "I'm so proud of my boys." He said this whether he was the coach or one of the players. He always thought of everyone as one of his boys.

After facing a loss, Mr. Skull sat quietly and told himself, "I'm still proud of my boys," over and over again until he was actually proud of his boys. Sometimes his wife would sit with him and he would lay his head on her chest while she patted his mostly hairless skull. He vowed to be a better person, not just as a football player or as a coach, but in the entirety of his life. There was no correlation between being a good person and winning at football, but it seemed as though there ought to be.

The child was drooling. One of the women wiped away the drool. Mrs. Skull went over to the girl and said, "Hi," in the most timid of voices. The girl would not look at her face, but instead stared off into the distance. Mrs. Skull was a patient woman. She had filed several hundred nonprofit grants in her lifetime. She stood in front of the girl asking her questions about her life and telling her about their family and how they were so excited to meet her. The girl said nothing. At one point, the child lifted one of her hands into the air and made a reaching gesture, causing Mrs. Skull to turn around and give Mr. Skull a smile, but after she put her hand down it was clear that the movement had been directed at the empty space in front of her rather than to Mrs. Skull.

Many of Mr. Skull's high school students had spent years of their lives living in refugee camps. They didn't have the language to tell him what this was like and it wasn't his place to ask. It was his job to teach them math and that's what he was good at. He drew symbols on the board. He said words like, "add and subtract," but these phrases were meaningless unless one could connect the sound to the action. He drew the symbols on the board like Bob Ross painted things for children on the television show his kids had watched when they were younger. Though Mr. Skull was a football coach, he never yelled. Yelling was not a way to create understanding. He drew the symbols repeatedly on the overhead projector and the teenagers loosely mimicked these symbols on their tests as though they were his art students and accuracy didn't matter.

The women took the child away. She was tired, they said, but Mr. Skull was uncertain as to how they knew. What was the sign for tired in this child's language? Had she blinked a particular blink that Mr. Skull, so captivated by his wife's attempts to get the girl to respond, had failed to notice?

"Can she communicate?" Mr. Skull asked the women. Earlier their English had been competent, but their answer came slowly like they too were losing the ability to speak. The answer came as a conglomeration of voices, all of them women, coming together to form a single sentence. "Sometimes we think she understands what we are saying," they said.

"How do you know she understands?" he asked, but they had no answer to that question.

That night in the hotel room Mrs. Skull laid her head on Mr. Skull's chest. "I love her even though she didn't speak to me," she said. One of the reasons Mr. Skull loved Mrs. Skull was her deep and unabashed ability to love. Out of all the reasons he loved her, this was the most selfish. He wanted to be loved like that, wholly and completely. "I know," Mr. Skull said, and smoothed her dyed blonde hair.

They visited her one last time. "There is still a chance," Mr. Skull told himself when it was the fourth quarter and he was losing a football game and what he told himself when he was going to leave a child that had almost been his child in Russia forever.

She was throwing a tantrum and it was almost a relief to see her like that, emotional and human, instead of the badly-shaped wax figurine of the day before. The women were trying to comfort her. They offered toys and food and attempted to hug her, but there was no consoling this child who screamed as though she knew she was being left behind. The women apologized. "She gets like this sometimes," they said. They took her away quickly.

Mr. Skull told Mrs. Skull to wait outside with the children while he told the women at the orphanage that they couldn't take the child. "We don't have the necessary resources," he said.

Mr. Skull and Mrs. Skull took their children to a park nearby their hotel and the children were happy that the playground had much of the same equipment that they were used to playgrounds having in the United States. To leave home and only look for what is familiar.

Mr. Skull's classroom smelled when he returned. When he pointed this out to his colleagues, they laughed and said, "Skull, that's what teenagers smell like."

The trial had started for the football player, the one that had raped the women. Because he was a minor, they weren't allowed to show pictures of his face, but Mr. Skull already knew what he looked like. A man identified by block letters on the back of a jersey.

The football player had an alibi, but not the sort of alibi that meant he had not done it, but rather he had an explanation for why he had. He had been smoking marijuana those two nights and everyone knew that marijuana wasn't the sort of drug to go and make a kid rape somebody and especially not two somebodies, but the stuff he was smoking had been laced with something, PCP, he said.

Mr. Skull had smoked weed in college. He liked to go out on the weekend and party with the other players. He did this dance, a Skull dance, where he went bounce, bounce, bounce, chug beer, bounce, bounce, bounce. He had a lot of body to move. At the end of the night he went back to Mrs. Skull's little dorm room who was then Not-Yet-Mrs.-Skull. Her dorm room was so much nicer than his own dorm room and they had sex on her little bed and she fell asleep on top of him because there was nowhere else for her to sleep. She told him, Skull, that his body was like a pillow.

The accused rapist's grandmother assured the press that her grandson had done no such thing, even though he had confessed. "He's such a good athlete," she said repeatedly. "I don't know why they are blaming him for this. It could've been anybody."

The students started acting up in the springtime. That's what the teachers said in the break room, "The kids are acting up again. It's that springtime weather," and then they laughed like they made a joke. The entire back row of Mr. Skull's geometry class had been sleeping for weeks. He caught a boy openly reading *Harry Potter* instead of looking at his math book.

"Do you want to see real magic?" Mr. Skull asked. "Pay attention in math class."

One day Mr. Skull stopped teaching in the middle of a lesson and told the class about his trip to Russia. "We just didn't have the resources necessary," he said. Then he, Mr. Skull, began to cry in front of everyone and they, the students, stared up at him with the same blank faces they always did and Mr. Skull realized that these were not the faces of misunderstanding as he'd always assumed, but just how their faces looked, smooth and expressionless. The impossibility of reading a face: what could a nose tell a person anyway?

That night, Mr. Skull found a wart on one of Mrs. Skull's toes. He asked her where she had gotten it from and was she seeing other men and Mrs. Skull patted him on the head and said, "No, honey. It's probably from the gym."

Mr. Skull was acquainted with grimy locker room floors, the fungus that can grow between the toes. Humans like a plot of land ripe for fertilizing. "We should burn that off," he told Mrs. Skull.

Mr. Skull applied for a job as a math teacher/head football coach at a different high school. He liked the sound of it, Coach Skull, Head Coach.

They called him in for an interview a week later and offered him a job on the spot. They shook hands at the end of the meeting and said, "Pretty weird about that trial, eh?" He said, "Yeah, pretty weird."

The accused rapist was found guilty and sentenced to two terms of twenty-three years. At Mr. Skull's goodbye party held in the break room at the high school where they served cupcakes with a skull and crossbones on them and made jokes about how they would see him on the football field next year, everyone murmured how good it was that such a bad man had been put behind bars. But, they added, they still never suspected that he could've done such a thing. He was such a good football player.

Mrs. Skull took the picture of the girl down from the refrigerator, but she didn't throw it away and instead put it in a box of pictures they had from when the biological Skull children were babies and people still occasionally got pictures developed.

Tommy Skull was doing well at little league baseball. He was one of the biggest kids on the field. Mr. Skull was careful to cheer for all the children on the field, but admitted that he cheered the loudest for his son. One of the team mothers asked if he could "please keep it down a bit" and he looked at her and said. "It's a sports game."

At his new job, Mr. Skull had his own office with his name on the door. "Skull," it said. The office was in a basement and had cinderblock walls, but Mr. Skull couldn't complain. They couldn't afford to give him a nice desk chair—they were a public school after all—so Mr. Skull brought in his desk chair from home. When no one was looking, he would take a couple spins in the chair before coming to a stop in front of the computer.

"This is all I ever wanted," Mr. Skull said, looking around at the cinderblock walls and putting barbeque chips in his mouth. Mrs. Skull didn't like it when he ate chips. She wanted him to eat well-rounded meals for his health. "I need you to live a long time," she said. But Mr. Skull decided that he deserved to eat some chips that day. Mr. Skull had been losing weight. His bones starting to show through the skin.

The Yellow Facemask

She hadn't been planning to rob the bank. Her face was cold.

Or maybe she had been planning to rob the bank and her face was cold. Sometimes bank robbers feel a chill in their cheeks just like any ordinary person.

The facemask was yellow. She couldn't remember buying it or recall why she had chosen that color. There were a lot of yellow things in her closet: cardigans and dresses, a nightgown that bordered on an ugly green. She supposed at one time she must've enjoyed the color. Said things like, "Yellow is cheerful."

On that day however, yellow did not make her feel cheerful and instead made her feel like the top part of a banana, the knob that is peeled down to reveal the gushy insides.

It was one of those winter days that was so cold that the car door was frozen shut and Elise, with her small body and yellow-knob head was unable to open the door and had to return inside to get her husband who was still wearing his pajamas pants to come outside and open it for her.

"You're starting to turn into the chair, all brown and leather," she said to him.

"The chair leads a good life," he replied and looked up at her. "You look like a bank robber in that thing."

He had to put on his Gore-Tex jacket and boots just to go outside.

"Sure is cold out there," he said. "Are you sure you want to go out now?"

The streets were icy. The weather had warmed and then frozen again covering everything in a slippery transparent sheen. Elise used to be afraid of car accidents, of a broken skull, back, fender, but in the past couple of years had found herself developing a fearlessness that other people, her doctor and children included, labeled as forgetfulness. Whatever she was going to be, she was not going to be one of those women that clutched at the steering wheel with both hands.

She kept the facemask on in the grocery store. She found it comforting, the extra layer of yellow skin. No one knew that it was her underneath that mask and she was happy, for once, to be the person that was unrecognizable the way that so many people had since become unrecognizable to her. Her body was shapeless underneath the puffy winter coat. Even her hands were covered by her two-fingered extra-duty winter mittens that she normally wore just to shovel snow. The cold masks a lot of things. Her face was just one thing buried that day.

The grocery store workers said hello to her the way they always did. They asked her how she was doing, if she was finding everything she needed. She said nothing. She suddenly understood why there were women in some countries who covered their face every day.

She paid for her groceries with cash. She didn't like to use a credit card and she saw the way that people glared at her as she fumbled with her checkbook. Always fumbling in a way that made her doctors suggest some kind of dreaded degenerative disease. She had left her reusable grocery bags in the car because she always left her reusable grocery bags in the car. She wanted to be good to the environment, but like everything else that she wanted to be good to, she found herself lacking. She accepted the plastic bags and killed the earth a little more.

The bank was two blocks down from the grocery store. The bank parking lot made Elise nervous. There was one occasion, an occasion she tried not to think about, where she had accidently backed up into another car and dented their paneling. Her car was unscathed though, so she got back in and drove home. She spent the rest of the day crying and cleaning the house and waiting for the police to come get her. They never did. No one ever found out it was her. Since then she had always parked on the street, nervous that they would figure out that she was the one who did it, nervous that she would suffer a repeat performance.

As Elise walked into the bank she saw her reflection in the glass, a yellow-bulb head enlarged in its mirroring, puffy coat that doubled her body in size. She giggled. She did look like a bank robber. The thought was so absurd. No one would ever expect her, a mother, a wife, a homeowner, to rob a bank.

She giggled further as she scrawled a note on the deposit slip, "Give me money," in her looping cursive. She realized that she had inadvertently carried in her reusable grocery bags. Always armed with things at the wrong time.

There was no line. She walked up to the teller. She had seen her before, a young black girl. She wore a heavy sweater over a button-up shirt. She had a nametag that said "Jessica."

Elise passed her the note. She couldn't stop laughing. She couldn't wait to tell her husband about her joke when she got home.

Jessica, instead of issuing her normal instructions to run the debit card through the machine, had unlocked the cash register in front of her. It was then that Elise realized that Jessica actually thought she was a bank robber. She thought about correcting the mistake, but Jessica was already neatly stacking piles of bills. That's what Elise remembered about Jessica. She remembered the nice way that Jessica stacked money and handed it over with a smile. It made it feel like a present rather than a withdrawal from one's own account.

Jessica was not smiling that day. Elise knew what it was like to feel fearful of another person and thus she understood the look on Jessica's face, though Elise had only previously experienced that look from the inside. Elise had been afraid on the street, in bars, at the airport, in her home. Elise had been afraid everywhere a person could be afraid. To be on the other side, to make a person afraid, was something entirely different.

There had been previous times that Elise had felt powerful inside of her body. The men she had been with before her husband. The time she ran a community 5K. But she had never held a gun, never used her body as a weapon. No one had ever treated her as a threat before. No one had ever shoved money into reusable grocery bags at her behest, treated her as though she were something to be fearful of, something that could penetrate the skin. She realized that her two-fingered gloves resembled a gun. She almost clarified that they were only her hands, delicate with rings circling several fingers, but by then Jessica had handed her the bag.

Elise took the bag and ran. Elise did not know how to run. Elise ran very slowly. Surely they would catch her. Surely they would shoot her down, putting holes in her yellow-fabric skin. This would just be another occasion where she had failed. She made it to her car and sped home. She could hear sirens behind her, but they weren't chasing her. She pulled into the driveway and went inside. She decided to make cookies.

"These are the best cookies I've ever made," she exclaimed to her husband.

"You always make good cookies," he said.

Elise had never been filled with such love.

The second time she robbed a bank it was a purposeful act. It was summer. Her husband's skin, covered only by worn boxers with holes where his legs met, stuck to the leather of his chair.

She was cleaning out the hall closet. Summer cleaning. They had so many things that she never remembered acquiring. Plaid scarf. Rain boots too small for anyone who lived in the house. Seven umbrellas. Elise never remembered to bring an umbrella with her when it was raining and would purchase another when she was out and vow to become a better umbrella user.

She had a cardboard banker's box in which she was collecting these unused items. Banker's boxes don't really have anything to do with banking. They are about taxes like anything else.

There was the coat Elise's husband wore only once a year when they went out and bought a Christmas tree from the YMCA Christmas tree sale. A coat that she had bought her daughter that her daughter never wore. Elise's daughter had always valued saving feelings over saving money, though in the long run she had not saved anything at all.

Elise put on the coat. It was too small for her, the middle buttons unable to close around her breasts. Breasts another thing on the list of things that Elise once cherished that she now wished to put in a banker's box and donate to Goodwill.

The coat was corduroy. Elise had thought it cute. It was on sale. The trick of sales was that they convinced people to buy things they didn't really need under the guise of a lower price. Elise was very susceptible to such ploys. Her hall closet evidence as such. Eight different hats. Seven gloves without their partner. A canister of tennis balls without any tennis balls inside of it. A swimsuit. A spider carcass.

The top no longer fit on the banker's box. Elise kept the coat on. She did not believe in giving something new away. She had her husband carry the box out to the car.

"Put some pants on," she said. It embarrassed her when her husband went out like that. Pants were made to cover thighs like his.

"It's too hot," he replied.

He was no longer good at lifting things and had to pick the box up and set it down several times before making to the car. Elise told herself not to be so critical. She was no longer good at the things that she used to be good at either. Sewing. Cheerfulness. Paying bills on time.

The air conditioner no longer worked in the car. It would cost too much to fix, so Elise rolled down the windows and turned up the fan.

"My own personal sauna," she said.

The yellow facemask was sitting on top of the pile of stuff. In a different box in a different closet Elise had a picture of a very old boyfriend. She had remained in contact with this man for several years after she married her husband and once had sent him a picture that she had taken of herself in her underwear. She had to take the film to a different city to be developed. She never showed her husband the pictures or told him about the ex-boyfriend and eventually they lost contact. Elise supposed it was possible that he was dead. The facemask was like a lover that could resurface at any moment. Something that had many possibilities or perhaps none at all.

Elise had never shown her husband the money. Based off his behavior for the entirety of their marriage, this was how she understood money was to be handled.

Elise did not know how to get the cash from underneath her bed into her bank account. It was not as though she could go into the bank and ask for it to be deposited. She bought petty things. Ice cream cones, a new hand lotion. Even if she could deposit it she did not know what she would buy. She idly considered a boat though there were no lakes nearby, though her body was not spry enough for boating.

Elise did not like going into Goodwill. Because the store was both the name of a corporation and an adjective, she was certain that this dislike implied a badness of self. The store made her itch though she touched no products once inside. Many of the women browsing the crowded racks of clothing were around her own age, and like her were wearing clothing that didn't fit and she suspected this was why she didn't like it. Something too close to her own skin.

Elise dropped the banker's box on the counter. The yellow facemask stared up at her.

"I think I'm going to keep this, actually," she said pulling it out of the box. The eyeholes looked at her reproachfully, aware that she had almost let it go.

She was thanked for her donation. Elise made some joke about the ever-replenishing nature of her hall closet.

She put the mask on in the car. It nearly suffocated her in the summer heat. She realized how improperly dressed she was: an old pair of jeans that she wore for cleaning, a jacket that didn't fit, and the yellow facemask.

She then drove to the bank and told everyone to put their hands in the air. They all obliged. She never felt so powerful.

Elise, in those small moments she allowed herself to remember her past robbery, had masturbated to the thought, her own fingers like the gun in the air, her own fingers like the gun inside of herself. She had not expected to do it again, but she also did not know how she would never do it again and thus it was unsurprising to find herself that way, facemask covering her skin.

The difference between wearing a facemask in the summer and wearing a facemask in the winter was that in the winter people assumed the wearer of the facemask wanted to protect themselves from the cold and in the summer everyone assumed the wearer of the facemask was robbing a bank. Neither of these assumptions were wrong. Elise was wearing a facemask and she was robbing a bank.

Jessica wasn't working. Elise hoped that Jessica had found a better job somewhere else. She had been an exceptionally good teller. This time there was a young man shoveling bills into a bag. A banker's bag. He was a very handsome young man, but he didn't handle the bills with the same crispness that Jessica did.

Elise had injured her hip in March while shoveling the sidewalk during a late winter storm. Women her age were not supposed to shovel sidewalks, or so the doctor said.

"How else will I have my requisite hip injury?" she asked and then laughed at her own joke. The doctor didn't laugh. The doctor told her it was best not to have any hip injuries at all.

In order to run, she had to put all of her weight on her right leg and then swing her left leg around in front of it. This action did not look like running at all. This action looked more like some kind of dance with a bag full of money, which actually describes many types of dancing.

She tripped on the curb that led in into the parking lot and lay on the ground for several minutes before she was able to lift herself again.

She could hear the sirens approaching. This was familiar. The way they had approached when she fell and broke her hip. That time her daughter had threatened suicide. When her husband had a heart attack that turned out to be a panic attack. When her son had fallen off the jungle gym and broken his arm.

It was possible that she could be caught. She could not imagine a way for herself to escape. She imagined having the yellow facemask stripped from her head to reveal the self below. Have her little body shoved against the sidewalk, handcuffs around her wrists.

Elise pulled herself up. The police cars had still not arrived. Elise was not one to believe in miracles, though this was not the only implausible thing that had happened in her life. The bag was heavy. Paper was always heavier than she expected in to be. Elise made it to the car. She threw the bag in the passenger seat of the car.

"Be calm," paramedics always said. The least comforting of phrases.

"Be calm," Elise murmured to herself as she got in the driver's seat. She drove away like someone who was not making a getaway. She drove away like she was just running errands. She saw a flash of police lights in her rearview mirror stopped in front of the bank. They did not chase after her. They did not suspect her little car or her little body peering over the dashboard. It was like they couldn't see her at all. She was both visible and invisible inside of the facemask.

Elise was hungry. She wanted some pancakes. She took off the facemask. Hot air blew at her from the vents. It felt nice after the cold of the bank.

"Trying to stop the gold from melting," she joked. She checked her reflection in the rearview mirror to make sure her lipstick wasn't smudged. It wasn't, but it had started to fill in the cracks in her skin.

She drove to the diner and parked her car. She was still wearing her daughter's jacket. She supposed it was her jacket now as she had worn it more than her daughter ever had. She went inside and sat in one of the plastic booths. She was glad for the warmth from the too-short sleeves. Elise never understood why they made restaurants so cold. Who wanted to be cold while they were eating?

"I want a tall stack," she said to the waiter.

"With chocolate chips," she added as he walked away.

She smothered the cakes in maple-syrup-colored corn syrup. She cut through each of the layers, spearing all three pancakes at once. The bites barely fit in her mouth. She couldn't remember the last time she had been so ravenous for something so sweet.

She left the server a pile of crumpled bills on the table. She left with crumpled bills spilling out of her pocket. She had chocolate smeared across her lips. People excused such blemishes on the face at her age.

On the Hunt

The crusties got to him in the park across the street. Alexis knew it was wrong to blame a dog for running away because the dog didn't know any better but she couldn't help but feel her heart ping when she opened the door and found that Franklin was missing.

Franklin was used to traveling. They had hopped from town to town and traversed deep into deserts and forests together. He was already adjusted to the transient lifestyle when the crusties took him and after she was no longer mad at his momentary desire to leave her, she blamed herself for all those times she had left him with friends in order to pursue her own financial endeavors.

A man emailed her. It had to be a man. A woman would've never gone up to the crusties and explained that they had seen a picture of that very same dog, Franklin, on Craigslist with a desperate plea for his return. A woman would've run as soon as the crusties said, "I'm going to keep him."

There are certain advantages to having an animal over engaging in a romantic relationship with another human. Alexis had once had a two-year relationship with a man and then had left him in order to go on an extended trip through the wilderness. She loved a woman briefly. And then there was Franklin. A dog never pointed out their owner's deficiencies the way a human might, but a human would never run away and be kidnapped by a group of crusty street punks the way that her dog was. There was no such thing as love without risk.

Alexis was a small woman. There was nothing especially feminine about her appearance. She had short hair and wore the same clothes camping that she did in her city life. Sometimes it was assumed that less feminine women had less to fear from men, though nothing about her life experience had ever proven this to be true. To be a woman of any type was to invite harassment and commentary from strangers. This was what stopped her from going after the roving pack of crusties then. A gendered restriction of a type that she had never encountered before.

"Go to the police," people told her. But Alexis knew the sort of things that could happen in police altercations and how sometimes bullets went where they weren't meant to go and how reporting could make things harder than they ever needed to be. Instead, Alexis decided to go hunting.

Alexis had once read a book that argued that humans, while not built for speed, had evolved in order to chase down prey animals on the hunt. Alexis didn't think she could ever chase down an antelope, but Alexis wasn't trying to chase down an antelope. She was trying to chase down a crust punk.

Alexis brought her friend Hannah along with her. One summer, Hannah had walked the entire length of the Appalachian Trail with all of her supplies on her back. In some ways, this sounded harder than trying to catch a herd mammal with bare hands.

Alexis had never before gone looking for someone that was homeless. Homeless people were ubiquitous. The crusties were different from other groups of homeless in that to them, homelessness was an aesthetic. To live like that was a choice until it wasn't.

They found a group of them clustered in downtown, a whole dreaded mass of them, dogs gathered at their feet. It was hard to differentiate Franklin from the other dogs and Alexis worried that maybe he had changed. Maybe he liked his life better with the crusties. To get him back, similar to fetching any living thing, was an act of selfishness. Of course, that was already inherent in her ownership of him.

Alexis had meant to approach them gently. She had meant to use reason. Instead, she started running. Hannah followed suit, trailing behind her. Alexis had never been a self-described "runner" until there was something she wanted back. She ran and the crusties started running too. They were used to such adjustments. Franklin ran with them. He was, after all, biologically inclined to be part of a pack.

"Franklin!" she yelled. "Franklin!" It was her voice that made him turn, start pulling on the leash toward her. The crusties dragged him along. Hannah was slow, her breath heavy. Alexis was on her own. She had never had such a moment where her body was so in control of her fate. "Franklin!" she yelled again.

When they finally ran together, they crashed. He, on his hind legs, hugging her. He smelled and she didn't care because that wasn't the sort of thing that mattered when a great love was returning. His ribs had grown underneath his skin, a bonyness that hadn't existed before.

Back at her apartment, she fed him treat after treat. Dog snacks. A banana with peanut butter. She gifted him new toys. She did it because she missed him. She did it because he had left and she thought that if she gave him enough then maybe he would never leave again.

Charlize with Many Hands

Charlize hadn't meant to become a stalker amongst many other things she hadn't meant to be: a smoker, a drinker, an occasional weed user, a binge eater. She told herself that her minor aberrations were within the norm. Everyone was allowed to behave badly sometimes, let loose.

Charlize worked as a hairstylist. Charlize was the woman who cut Lisa's hair. Lisa and Charlize had a lot in common. They were both women. They both had husbands and houses and they both had hair growing out of their heads. Of course, Charlize had these things in common with most of her clients. There was nothing special about Lisa.

Charlize and Lisa both shopped at the local food co-op. Lisa was a part owner and Charlize was not. That was okay. The local co-op was a store open to everyone. This was the first place that Charlize ran into Lisa outside of Georgio's Hair Salon. Lisa greeted Charlize by name. That was the thing about hairstylists: everyone always knew the name of the stylist they liked most.

"Just going to follow you everywhere you go," Charlize joked, trailing Lisa to the checkout. They said goodbye to each other and then ran into each other for the rest of the visit, rendering the initial goodbye obsolete. Lisa had a lot of greens in her cart. Charlize didn't know all the names of the greens that Lisa had. Charlize had two bottles of sparking water, an organic frozen pizza, and seven containers of organic Greek yogurt. While Lisa was checking out, Charlize eavesdropped on her membership number and used it at all of her subsequent visits to the co-op. "Yes, I'm Lisa," Charlize said when the crunchy granola co-op cashiers asked.

Charlize loved her husband more than anyone she had met before her husband. That was the problem with love: how was she supposed to know who she loved the most before she had loved everyone she possibly could? It was possible that there were people she would love more than her husband sometime in the future. Though she dreaded that possibility, she was open to it. Some things weren't meant to last forever. Charlize's husband was from Saudi Arabia and she loved this about him. She loved pulling her fingers through the thick black hair that grew all over his body.

Charlize and her husband had no children, but they did have a series of cats. Charlize collected the leftover hair from Georgio's Hair Salon and sewed cat toys in the shape of mice, using the hair as filler. Sometimes the cats ripped the seams of the toys open and hair would spill all over the floor. Charlize didn't mind because she loved sweeping human hair into the dust pan. It was one of the reasons she had become a hairstylist. There was something intimate about having other people's hair scattered all over her floor.

Because Charlize and Lisa went to the same grocery store, Charlize suspected that they lived close to each other. Because Lisa had been coming to see Charlize for some time, Charlize knew that Lisa had three children. It wasn't as though she had been looking for Lisa, but perhaps she had been looking for Lisa because whenever Charlize passed a yard in the neighborhood with three children in it Charlize scanned the yard for Lisa's familiar head of hair. Lisa and Charlize lived in a diverse neighborhood with many families. It was a nice place to be.

Charlize suspected that Lisa did not love her husband as much as Charlize loved her husband. For all her flaws, Charlize was very committed in her love. Lisa was constantly talking about her children. Denise was doing this and Scott was doing that and Brian was doing both this and that. Lisa rarely talked about her husband. This made Charlize suspicious of her love.

On one visit to Georgio's Hair Salon Lisa reported that her identity had been stolen. Having one's identity stolen only means having numbers that represent one's access to money stolen, of course. It had nothing to do with an actual identity. Lisa was still Lisa and she still needed her roots dyed and her bangs trimmed. She apologized, she was going to have to pay with a check. Charlize smiled. "No problem," she said. A lot of people paid with checks at Georgio's Hair Salon because no one liked getting their hair done more than old ladies and no one liked paying with checks more than old ladies did. That was how Charlize got Lisa's address.

Charlize and her husband liked to take walks after dinner. It was how they fit exercise in their busy lives. While they walked they held each other's hands and talked about their days. Charlize liked to describe her clients to her husband and her husband liked to describe the cars that he worked on as an auto mechanic to Charlize.

Charlize didn't alter their walking route to go by Lisa's house except maybe she did because Charlize looked up where Lisa lived on the internet and suggested to her husband that perhaps they ought to walk down a street they had never walked down before. Charlize's husband wasn't suspicious because he knew that Charlize loved him very much. Charlize's husband said that he would appreciate the change in scenery.

The first time Charlize saw Lisa's husband he was throwing a ball in the front yard to three children. Charlize knew they were named Brian, Scott, and Denise. Charlize presumed that Lisa was inside the house. Charlize presumed that Lisa was making a dinner composed of greens. Charlize could tell that Lisa's husband ate a lot of greens because he was very thin and fit and threw the ball very well. Charlize's husband was quite fat. She told him she didn't care. This was a lie.

Charlize started running into Lisa's husband at the food co-op. She put lots of greens in her cart because she knew this was what he liked. She once asked him a questions about cheeses that he didn't know the answer to. "You must have kids," she commented when he put bunny-shaped organic crackers in his cart.

Charlize knew that Lisa's husband worked in an office building because she followed him to work one Monday when Georgio's Hair Salon was closed. She tried to follow him inside the building as well, but they asked for her building ID and all she had were her Georgio's Hair Salon business cards so she gave the security guards a couple of those and left.

Charlize's husband knew that she had an independent streak in her. When they met, Charlize had purple hair with bleach-blonde highlights. She was always cutting and dying her hair, a constant reimagining of the self. Charlize's husband said that he had never seen anyone more beautiful in his life. Sometimes, when Charlize's hair was too short or too damaged, he let Charlize cut and dye his hair. He didn't care if she made him look silly, he said. All he wanted was for her to be happy.

After work, Lisa's husband went to a franchise gym and performed small acts of cardio and weightlifting. Charlize was not a gym person. She had said "gym person" with a derogative tone a multitude of times to various clients who were also not gym people. Charlize signed up for a membership at the franchise gym and followed Lisa's husband from machine to machine. Charlize started to get very fit.

Charlize's husband was often covered in oil and grease from working on cars all day. It didn't matter how many times he washed his hands, he was still dirty. Charlize worried that his skin was absorbing the oil, that he would start to be oily on the inside too. Charlize's husband told her not to worry. He suggested that she invite one of her friends for a drink. It had been awhile since she had seen anyone.

Sometimes instead of going to the gym after work Lisa's husband went to a bar. It took a while for Charlize to figure this out. She didn't know how to work out without Lisa's husband. She lost all coordination between her body and the machine. It was while on a girl's night out with her friend Marissa that Charlize spotted him, Lisa's husband, drinking a beer at the bar. He seemed to be alone, but he was chatting with the bartender. Charlize couldn't hear what he was saying, but she imagined he was talking about sports.

Charlize hadn't seen Lisa at Georgio's Hair Salon for several weeks. She worried she had been caught following Lisa's husband around the gym. She told herself this was silly, she hadn't done anything wrong. She was trying to get into shape, be healthy. Then she began to worry that something was wrong with Lisa. She imagined cancer, a death in the family, sudden rapid hair-loss.

"I'm worried about one of my clients," Charlize told her husband. He loved how much she cared about her clients at Georgio's Hair Salon. Sometimes he commented that she was more like a counselor than a hairstylist. "I'm both," she said. "A hairstylist has to have many hands."

Lisa returned with grown-out hair and an apology. Things had gotten so busy. Soccer season had just started and all of the kids had practice at different times. "I feel like a chauffeur," she complained. Charlize felt bad for Lisa. If only her husband would help out and drive the kids to practice sometimes then Lisa's hair wouldn't have formed the shape of a mullet.

One day Charlize had shown up at the gym to find it void of Lisa's husband. Instead of trying to drag herself through the ritualized movements, Charlize decided that she deserved a drink and went to bar down the street. She hadn't known that Lisa's husband would be in there or maybe she did because on several previous occasions she had watched him enter that particular establishment while sitting in her car. Charlize sat several stools down from Lisa's husband and ordered a margarita. "Haven't I seen you somewhere before?" Lisa's husband said. He was drinking a beer. Very masculine.

Charlize spent hours a day staring in the mirror. There were many moments when she found herself looking at her reflection rather than down at the hair she was cutting. That was okay, her fingers knew what to do. Hair cutting was more tactile than anything else. When Lisa's husband asked if he had seen her somewhere before Charlize made a puzzled expression. She didn't need a mirror to tell her that was how her face looked. "Do you go to my gym?" he asked. Her face lit up. "That must be it," she said.

Lisa's husband started saying hello to Charlize whenever he saw her. He didn't know her name. They weren't close like that yet. "I run into you everywhere," Lisa's husband said over the citrus section of the co-op. "The oranges look delicious today," Charlize replied. He waved to her reflection in the floor-length gym mirror and Charlize's reflection waved back. She started to feel self-conscious for the first time about her curvaceous figure.

Charlize's husband had to return to Saudi Arabia for a short visit. His father had died. Charlize stayed behind. They couldn't afford the loss of both of their incomes and besides, someone had to look after the cats. "You know how men are about their fathers," Melissa told Charlize over happy hour. "I know," she said. "I just don't like being in the house while he's gone."

Charlize had always preferred abnormal colors for her hair. Pink, purple, green, bleach blonde. She liked asymmetrical haircuts. She thought they better showed off her eyes. While her husband was gone, she dyed her hair a medium brown and had one of the other hairstylists at Georgio's Hair Salon cut her hair short. "You look like a mom," the other stylist joked. "I'm trying to tone down my look," Charlize replied.

At the gym, Charlize ran into Lisa's husband while he was refilling his water bottle. "Hey, you," he said. Charlize didn't mean to invite Lisa's husband to dinner, but maybe she did because she asked Lisa's husband if he would like to go to dinner at a nearby Mexico restaurant. "They serve all organic food," she said. This was a lie. Lisa's husband laughed and flashed his wedding band. "I'm married," he said. "I have three kids." Charlize showed him the sparkling diamond on her finger. "I'm married too," she said.

At the Mexican restaurant Charlize ordered a taco salad to impress Lisa's husband with her familiarity with greens. Lisa's husband ordered four tacos and a side of queso. He loved queso, he said, and his wife never wanted to eat it because she was always worried about her weight. Charlize nodded. She knew what Lisa looked like. She imagined Lisa at home, preparing dinner for Brian, Scott, and Denise. Lisa's husband had called her and said that he "ran into an old friend" and that they were "going to catch up over dinner." Charlize heard Lisa's familiar voice on the phone. Heard Lisa complaining about how tired she was.

After consuming three margaritas and a bowl of fried ice cream Charlize invited Lisa's husband back to her house. She was drunk, which gave her an automatic clause of unreliability in her actions. "My husband is out of town," she said. "He has some business that he's taking care of." It didn't take much pressure for Lisa's husband to agree to go back to Charlize's house. This was how she knew that he was unhappy in his marriage. Charlize's husband would never go home with someone so quickly.

When naked, Lisa's husband looked like he ate a lot of greens. Charlize could feel all of his ribs and his hipbones left a bruise on her inner thigh. She appreciated the way that he didn't murmur any of the ordinary clichés about how he "never did this" or how he "loved his wife." She suspected this was because he often did this and did not love his wife. He did, like Lisa, love Brian, Scott, and Denise. He told Charlize all about their most recent soccer tournament, a story that Charlize had already heard from Lisa and she grew quite bored while listening. "I think you should go," she said. She wondered if he often did this, stayed out late in another woman's bed. He did not appear to be wracked with guilt in the way that he pulled up his pants, looped the belt into the buckle, tucked the shirt in as though it had never been untucked. On the way out he took one of Charlize's business cards from her dresser. He made a joke about letting her style him in the future. She smiled. "Any time," she said and let him out the front door.

Charlize did not mean to call in sick to work or maybe she did because she picked up the phone and let out a little fake cough and said that she couldn't come in. She didn't want to get her germs all over her clients' hair. This was not the first time she had called in sick when she wasn't really sick, but everyone called in sick to work sometimes. Everyone needed a day off to take care of themselves.

Charlize got in her car and drove by the soccer field. She said she was driving by the soccer field on the way to the grocery store, though her refrigerator was full, though she stopped her car in the parking lot of the soccer field and the smallness of it stood out against all those mini-vans and SUVs, cars intended to hold a family, to keep a family safe from any trauma on the roads. Charlize did not even know if Brian, Scott, and Denise were on the field, except she did know, except that Lisa's husband had told her all about it the night before. Charlize knew everywhere those children went.

The field was filled with children in matching shirts of various colors. They walked around sucking on juice boxes and orange slices and eating granola bars. There was so much eating in children's soccer. Charlize's husband liked to watch soccer on television. Sometimes she sat with him while he did this because he liked it when she was sitting next to him. Charlize was never able to get into the sport, which was composed of almost-made opportunities. Her husband screaming at the television repeatedly that they had almost made it, almost gotten a goal, if only everything had gone differently they would've scored points. To Charlize, the children on the field were not much different than the grown men, their hair wild in the wind, their passes almost, but not quite, sufficient.

Charlize was not looking for Brian, Scott, and Denise until she found them. Brian clad in green, Scott in turquoise, and Denise in salmon. They had been momentarily abandoned by Lisa and her husband who were talking to another couple, other soccer parents, over by a container of plastic water bottles. Charlize could not judge them for this lapse in parenting. There were many parents on the field and many children left unattended. Who would suspect that it would be their children who stood together in a protective grouping that would be the ones that would be taken?

It was not hard for Charlize to lure Brian, Scott, and Denise to her car. She told them that she was a talent scout for the United States soccer team. She had watched them play, she said. They had a lot of potential. She wanted to introduce them to the coach. They would be back in a minute, she said. Their parents would not even notice that they were missing. The children, the little idiots, followed her to her car. They piled in the backseat, all three of them in a row. They were very excited, they told her, about their future careers as professional soccer players.

Charlize did not mean to cross state lines. Some lines that she had crossed were abstract, but the state line was literal. The children had started to complain. They wanted to know where the soccer coach was. They had not yet realized that Charlize was a fraud, that she knew nothing about soccer, that all she could do was style hair and make casual conversation. Soon, she told them, soon. Charlize had the same feeling as when she purposefully cut a client's hair too short, when she said "absolutely" to their requests and did the opposite. How far, she wondered, could she push it until they said something? Little clippings of hair floating down to the earth, covering the floor. Signs of her betrayal all around.

Love From Abby

He picked up the side job because he wanted to save money to buy an engagement ring. The common wisdom was that engagement rings should be three months' salary. Luke didn't know where these additional three months where he didn't pay the rent or the internet bill were supposed to emerge from and he didn't make all that much money at Uncle Paul's Fried Chicken shop to begin with.

There was no Uncle Paul and there was no Abby. Luke thought that Paul sounded more like a senator than someone's uncle that made chicken. Luke had invented an entire life for Paul. He had a wife who was very fat from all the chicken. That's why Paul made fried chicken so much: he liked his wife fat, voluminous. They had three children. Sometimes, on accident, Luke said "chickens" instead of "children" and Joe, the French fry guy, said "Yo, that's sick dude. That means they eat their own kids" and Luke said, "Maybe they do." Unlike the wife, the children were all very thin and aspiring dancers. Dancing was a way for them to rise out of the coop of the chicken business. On some days, Luke liked to imagine that he was having an affair with Uncle Paul's wife. She was a very sensual woman.

Abby was in the title of the texting service, Love From Abby. Luke didn't know that there wasn't an Abby, so he didn't invent one. He liked to respect the realness of others' lives. He didn't think he was qualified to write about love, but at a certain point he hadn't been qualified to fry chicken and that hadn't stopped him from applying to Uncle Paul's Fried Chicken. It turned out that all it took to fry chicken was to coat it in a mixture of egg and flour and submerge it in the deep fryer. Writing about love was much the same.

Love From Abby was a texting service for busy professionals. Sometimes people were too busy at their day jobs to send messages to their significant others. Things like, "Hello" or "I miss you" or "I hope your day is going well" or "I can't wait for tonight." Luke couldn't imagine being so busy. Since Paul didn't actually exist, there was very little oversight at Uncle Paul's Fried Chicken and Luke spent more time scrolling through his phone than he did frying the chicken.

Luke didn't have to invent lives for the busy professionals because the busy professionals filled out forms all about themselves. Love From Abby offered several different packages starting at one text per day and capping out at forty texts per day. The busy professionals detailed the level of commitment (just getting to know each other, committed, spouse), how affectionate they typically were (matter of fact, sweet, adoring), and the basic facts surrounding the courtship. They also included a picture of their significant other so the Love From Abby employees could compliment them as well.

Luke was in love with a woman named Erica. Luke and Erica had only known each other four months, but Luke knew it was love after he got the stomach flu and was sick out of both ends at the same time and Erica still had sex with him a few days later. Erica worked for a public relations firm. The firm was very busy promoting their newest client, Dirty Sam's, a nightclub that had just opened downtown. Part of Erica's job was going downtown on Friday and Saturday nights and encouraging men that were walking around to go into Dirty Sam's instead of one of the other nightclubs in the downtown area. For this reason, Luke and Erica were only able to see each other on weeknights, and then only on the days when Erica wasn't too tired. Luke said that he didn't mind, he knew it was important for her career. He did mind though. He wanted to see Erica every day. If it were possible for him to merge his body with hers like romantic Siamese twins, he would've.

The application for Love From Abby was a short writing test. Luke hadn't excelled in English in college or in any other subject. "Man, what do you need a college degree for working here?" Joe the fry guy asked him once and Luke had no argument. By the time that people were old enough to choose what they wanted to do with their lives, it was already too late and everything had already been decided for them. There were worse things than fried chicken though. At least Luke was no longer delivering pizzas.

The test was a series of hypothetical text messages with blank spaces to write in responses. To "How are you?" Luke wrote, "Good, just thinking about you." To "Do you want to get together tonight?" he said, "I can't tonight, but I will be holding my breath until I see you again." The interviewer told him that he was very romantic and he was just the type of employee they were looking for. "We want messages that convey a deep undying love and are also very neutral," she said.

Love From Abby was set up like a call center. Each employee had their own monitor where the texts were routed through the numbers of their clients. Luke asked his shift manager if he could hang up a picture of Erica at his desk and she said, "Sorry, the desks are shared between the night workers and the day workers and we have a rule against personal momentos."

Luke took the weekend shifts at Love From Abby. He was careful to separate his fried chicken clothes from the rest of his outfits, but everything ended up reeking of chicken anyway. Erica told him that she liked it and that it reminded her of her childhood. "I didn't know that you grew up on a chicken farm," Luke said and she didn't laugh. Erica ate a piece of the chicken once and then never ate any ever again. "It wouldn't be good for my job if I got fat," she said. The other employees at Love From Abby avoided Luke and his chicken smell. He said he was okay with it. He wasn't looking for love or friendship. He had Erica and he imagined that should be enough.

Love From Abby tried to keep their text messages as consistent as possible. When a new client enrolled in the program, they were assigned a team of message senders that took over their case. There were three main rules that it was important all messages embodied. 1) Never let the message receiver know that the person sending the messages is someone other who they think they're communicating with. 2) Never make in-person plans or agree to talk on the phone. 3) Make them feel so loved that they never need anything more than the messages. Luke spent the first half hour of every shift reading over the transcripts from the previous shifts. It was important to keep a consistent narrative. A person could only text "thinking about you" so many times a day before it started to seem insincere.

There were some clients that Luke liked better than others. There were some busy professionals that used Love From Abby as a replacement for their actual relationship. Love From Abby texted their significant others "I love you too," when they went to bed at night and "Good morning," when they woke up. It was Love From Abby that responded to their daily minutiae, who said, "I'm sorry, baby," when their car broke down. Who said, "It will be okay," when they were let go of their jobs. If they could avoid seeing each other in person, it was possible for their clients to go years without actually saying anything to their loves. One woman, Claudia, texted her husband over eighty times a day without realizing that it was never him responding. It was Luke or the weeknight version of Luke, Andy, or the weekday version of both of them, Keisha. All of them thought fondly of Claudia as if she were one of their own.

New client reports came in a manila folder with a picture of the love object clipped inside. Screenshots of previous text messages were printed as examples of grammar and tone. There was a lot of weight put into whether or not someone used a period. Proper grammar sounded cold when it came from someone who didn't ordinarily type that way. Most of their clients were men and most of the people they texted were women. Luke got the impression that these women were people the men used to love, a love that had since gone cold. He privately thought that it would be better to just break up with someone in that circumstance, but Love From Abby discouraged that type of things. They said it was important for the employees to regard their work as moral and relationship saving.

It was on a Saturday that Luke found his own picture. He had been scheduled for an early shift at Uncle Paul's Fried Chicken and the oil smell was particularly pungent when he sat down at his desk that day. He was pleased to see that there was a folder in the "New" stack. It got tiring texting the same people, especially when he was only pretending to be in love with them. He thought there had been some sort of mistake when he opened the folder. How had this picture of his face become clipped inside? He thought that perhaps it was a staff photo, though they had never taken one of those in his memory. Then he saw the text messages. Those endless confessions of love. "When can I see you?" he said and said and said. "I hope work is good tonight." "I love you." "Someday we won't be busy like this."

Luke had been working at Love From Abby long enough to know that he was one of the pathetic clients. One of the people they made fun of in the break room. The guy who didn't realize that he was being played. He was lucky in that the weekday staff never interacted with the weekend staff in person and only communicated through text. This meant that when Andy and Keisha sent him messages, they sent them as though he were just another sad recipient of their services. Luke, after all, was a common enough name and he hadn't been able to leave any physical identifiers at their shared desk space. Luke should've broke up with Erica then, but surely if she had enrolled in Love From Abby then she still felt something for him. It wasn't cheap to pay for someone else to send text messages to your boyfriend. Erica was the busy professional that Love From Abby was always talking about:

someone truly in love that didn't have time to send text messages. Luke closed the folder and entered his number and Erica's number within the system. He sent her a text message and it showed up in the system, "How are you today?" he asked her and himself. "Good," she said. Luke knew this was accurate because this was always what she said when he asked. His phone vibrated with the response. His body tingled a little.

He should've stopped texting Erica, but it was so hard to fill the time between deep frying at Uncle Paul's Fried Chicken. He tried downloading a popular cell phone game and ended up spending over a hundred dollars before he deleted the game off his phone. Intellectually, he knew he wasn't talking to Erica. When he got to work, he could see entire transcripts of conversations they had and yet, it felt like he was talking to her. The messages sounded like her and the feeling he got inside from reading them were the same feelings he got when Erica had actually said those things. Emotionally, there was no difference between a love that was real and love that was a lie.

He sent himself messages too. Things that Erica would never say. He knew that Keisha and Andy would read the messages and start to mimic his language. If he said, "I love you more than the earth," then they would be forced to come up with other, similarly large sentiments. Luke wondered if they knew it was him. There was little overlap in their shifts and none of the employees liked to get too close to him because of his overwhelming chicken smell. If they knew it was him, he suspected they wouldn't be surprised. Who could love someone who smelled so much like chicken?

Luke had thought that there was no love that could surpass what he felt for Erica until he started communicating with himself pretending to be Erica. The new Erica was never hesitant to deliver compliments. The new Erica said things like, "When we get married." The new Erica wanted to honeymoon in Jamaica. The new Erica was dreaming of owning a stand mixer and baking for him when he became her husband. The new Erica didn't require a ring because the new Erica didn't have any fingers. The best thing about the new Erica was that she always texted him back. She was never withholding like the old Erica had been. The new Erica could never elude him because the old Erica was paying for the new Erica to be there.

Luke was two and a half months into his job at Love From Abby when Erica ended her service. In that time, he had been working nearly constantly and eating fried chicken almost exclusively, which had caused both his weight and his bank account to spike. He told himself that he would get back into shape after he quit his Love From Abby job. He would join the gym that Erica belonged to and they could attend fitness classes together. He thought that Erica ending her service was a signal that she was going to begin texting him again. The real Erica. Instead, two days later she called him and broke it off. It had been a long time since he'd heard her voice. It was almost nothing like he imagined it. Like she was never the girl that he'd fallen in love with in the first place.

Luke mourned the loss of Erica deeply. There was a day when he considered dropping his phone in the deep fryer, but Joe the French fry guy talked him out of it. "Honestly, dude? Erica sounded super lame," he said. It wasn't so much that Luke missed her body (though he did miss her body deeply), but rather he missed having someone to text with during the day while he fried chicken. He didn't know how to feel the hours of his life without the artifice of love.

Luke went to the phone store and got a second phone and a new number. He said it was a surprise for his girlfriend. He downloaded an application for Love From Abby from the website and uploaded a picture of him, a better one than Erica had sent in. It was expensive to do all this. Luke needed his second job at Love From Abby just to pay for his Love From Abby service. It was worth it though. Worth it as he stood over the deep fryer and could feel his phone in his pocket as he buzzed. The newest Erica asking how he was. The newest Erica so deeply in love. The newest Erica with him forever or until he cut off service to himself.

If I Kill You We Can't Be Together

I tell people that I didn't know when we met. It sounds better that way. It makes it sound like I was coerced into something. I like to think of myself in that way: pliable. Something ripe for the taking.

I first saw him at yoga class, his head dangling between his legs in downward-facing dog. I am always recognizing people incorrectly. I plaster faces from my memories onto the wrong bodies. I thought this was what happened with him. I thought only members of the bourgeoisie did yoga, though perhaps murderers can get into corpse pose better than the rest of us.

I struggled with my breathing for the rest of the class. To be honest, I always struggled with breathing. The most integral part of a yoga practice, life.

I imagined telling my girlfriends what I had seen over cocktails. "It was him, Carter Gregory," I would say. "The murderer." Too bad I never went for drinks with my girlfriends. We were busy and tired and no longer desperate for company the way that we'd once been. I told them things in my head that I would never say aloud to anyone. My crowded internal dialogue that made up for lack of human contact.

That was the best part about Carter. I could tell him anything and nothing would ever be worse than the things that he'd done.

I began hoping I would run into him. Where did killers hang out? Sex dungeons? Vampire Clubs? Hunting stores? No, it was 5 PM Vinyasa on Monday, Wednesday, and Friday. The class was crowded. He arrived after I did. I worried it was too auspicious to move my yoga mat directly next to his. I did it anyway. He could make a person abandon all reason without a single word.

There were five of them, women that he had killed. All of them were strangers, women that he'd approached on the street. It always started the same way: he asked if he could borrow their cellphone. His phone was dead and he was trying to meet up with a friend. All of the women said no. Of course they did. Who was so stupid as to let a stranger use their phone at night?

Their bodies were found in dumpsters around the city. Carter wasn't a complete idiot. He knew to spread out the evidence of his crimes. I once asked him if he still would've killed them had they let him use their cellphone. He didn't respond. He always said the same thing. "I'm innocent. I was acquitted," he said. "Only on a technicality," I reminded him.

The vagina was always a hole, but it was even more so on the women that he killed. "What did you put inside of them to make them that way?" I asked him. And he responded as he always did, "I'm innocent. I was acquitted." I gazed at him and said pointedly, "I know your dick isn't so large."

I struck up conversation with him the first time after a Wednesday night class. He was wearing boots, the kind that people wore hiking. They took a long time to lace up. I wondered if that's what he wore when he killed the women. There were never any footprints found. He didn't seem interested in talking, but one of his laces became tangled and I pressed the issue until he was staring at my breasts. We all have our ways of luring people into our grasp.

"She came onto me," he would say later. Too bad it was a cliché. Clichés sucked the truth out of things. I had come onto him, but it didn't matter.

He got off on a technicality. There were mistakes made in the collection of evidence. The DNA was thrown out of the case due to contamination. Pictures of the crime scene were lost. Police officers were fired. "There just wasn't enough to convict him," the jury said. It helped that he had a nice face. Baby face, people said.

Dating him went against my feminist sensibilities. I had read about women like myself before I knew I was one of them. There's a word for it, "hybristophilia." Women who love men that have done something terrible.

Carter had gotten a slew of letters during his time in jail. Women that had quit their day lives in order to watch the trial, the back of his head behind the witness table. He had a thick neck, skin pockmarked with ingrown hairs. "Emotionless" was the way the newspaper described his face.

It was rumored that his motives for the first killing were a slight by a girl in a bar and then he discovered that he liked it, the killing. I guess people don't know if they'll like something until they try it. That's how I felt about broccoli and running. I could understand partaking in something that once seemed grotesque.

He told me on the third date. He asked if I had seen coverage of the trial. I lied and said no. Of course I had. Everyone had. He was a misogynist with a capital M. The sort of man that kills women because he can't get a date. I was an avid reader of the newspaper until we officially became boyfriend/girlfriend and then I cancelled my subscription so that he wouldn't know how much I knew about it. They turned him off, the groupies. "I'm innocent though," he said. "I was acquitted."

On our fifth date, we went to see a slasher flick. It was his idea. It was disappointing what a stereotype he was. The yoga had suggested a personal depth that never revealed itself in other ways.

I had never previously been into the horror genre, but as the masked killer tore apart the screaming woman's body, I found myself turned on in a way that I'd never been turned on before. I'd never liked sex very much. It had always been dry and painful, something I did for my partner's pleasure. "Take me, take me!" I wanted to scream as the film played. I didn't though. I'd always been shy about vocalizing my desires.

"He's really very normal," I told people, cashiers, the yoga teacher, my coworkers, really anyone who would listen. I loved telling people that I was dating Carter Gregory, the acquitted serial killer. I hadn't thought I was thirsty for fame until I had it. I started dressing the way that I thought a serial killer's girlfriend should dress, in all black with a lot of cleavage.

I started to fanaticize about Carter killing me. I bought a gun and put it in my bedside drawer. "For protection," I told him. I hoped that he would take out the gun and shoot me with it, right then and there. Instead he said, "That's a good idea. I worry about you." It disappointed me that he didn't think about me the same way that he thought about those women he had killed. I started developing a collection of rare knives. I said I was taking up baseball in order to keep a bat by the bed.

I wrote, "I want you to kill me," in the fogged up mirror after my showers. I told him that I had gone to see my lawyer and drawn up a will. I asked him questions like, "Do you believe in God?" and "What do you think happens after we die?" He said, "Yes" and "We go to heaven." His coyness added to his charm.

"Do you love me?" I asked him one night. "I always feel like I love you more than you love me." He said, "Yes." He said, "I'm sorry you feel that way." We were spooning. I was always the big spoon even though his body was much larger. "If you love me," I said, "You would kill me the way that you killed those women." He was silent and then snored a little, asleep.

"If I kill you, we can't be together," he said. The tough conversation like a dam broken open in our relationship. It was annoying how practical he was. "Death is the truest eternity," I replied. I wasn't sure what it meant. I was always more interested in elegance in speech than meaning.

I wanted to inspire him the way that those women had. I cheated on him and told him, hoping it would inspire rage. Instead, he cried and cried, revealing an unflattering vulnerability. I ate all his favorite foods and smashed his favorite bottle of whiskey. He said, "We can always buy more."

In the end, I tricked him. I snuck out of the house in the middle of the night and put pillows in the bed to make it look like I was still sleeping. Outside, I smashed the glass in the backdoor as though I was breaking in. Carter heard the noise. He grabbed the gun. He grabbed the bat. He grabbed one of knives. He thought he was protecting me, those pillows in bed indistinguishable from my bones. I heard a gunshot. I felt my body falling. I felt an exquisite pain that I had never felt before. Like stubbing the toe over the entire body. My skull smashed in. My throat slashed. I heard him say, "No, no, no, not again." I dissipated into nothing before I could say, "This was all I ever wanted!" I dissipated into nothing before I could ask, "Was I your very favorite slaughtering?"

5 Bad American Habits I Broke While Traveling Through Europe

1. Let Go of Your Material Possessions

I spent months packing for the trip. My husband had just bought me new breasts. Thousands of dollars so that I would look like a European in Europe. A pair of double Ds pushed so high into the air that they nearly touched my chin. Wearing anything felt like wearing lingerie. There were a couple of times in Italy when they made me wear a plastic cover just to go into a church.

I got catcalled everywhere I went. At first I took it as a compliment. "Hey, pretty lady." "Hi, beautiful." Kissing sounds that followed me down the street. It's not a compliment. Don't ever think it's a compliment. Despite the thousands of dollars I had spent, everyone knew I was American. They knew before I opened my mouth. It didn't matter what I was wearing. I hadn't packed any blue jeans and then I was shocked to find that everyone around me wore blue jeans and it was me, in my expensive slacks and skirts, that stood out as the outsider. I was always wearing the wrong thing.

The waiters all spoke to me in English. They made me feel inarticulate. I wanted to practice my knowledge of French. I was a French minor in college but had since forgotten everything I'd learned. I purchased a series of miniature dictionaries before leaving, French, German, Italian, Spanish. I thought I could carry them around in my purse as a reference. Dictionaries, it turns out, are only useful for people who already know the language. It is difficult to make meaning by shouting a single word repeatedly.

I ended up leaving all of my dictionaries behind in a hotel in Munich. I was in a rush to catch my train. I kept confusing the hours after noon. What was 15:00? I kept trying to subtract two or twelve and only confused myself further. I realized my mistake while enjoying an afternoon liter of beer at a brauhaus. "Shit, shit, shit," I said, and everyone knew what I meant. I stuffed all of my nice shirts in my bag but left behind the dictionaries. I missed my train anyway. German trains always run on time.

2. Travel Alone

I had always wanted to go to Europe, my husband said. He bought me a plane ticket as a surprise for my birthday. We were at a restaurant. I was wearing a black sequined dress and heels. I'd been panicking for most of the day because I had a zit on my forehead and kept touching it, which only made it swell up larger. It was comforting to sit and eat pasta in the dark, candlelit room. I didn't normally allow myself to eat pasta, but because it was my birthday, I made an exception. I kept sneaking slices of bread to dip into the marinara sauce. It is still considered sneaking when a person is hiding something from themselves.

I smiled when I opened the card and saw the ticket, though I was actually thinking about my zit and wondering whether my husband could see it or not and if, after fourteen years, such a blemish could cause him to stop loving me. It turns out that he didn't even notice the zit, which might have been the only outcome worse than disgust.

I assumed he was going to go with me, along with our fourteen-year-old son, but he said no, it was a trip for me. Once the swelling went down in my chest, he put me on a plane with thousands of dollars of new clothes in brands that I thought I was pronouncing correctly but never really was, and told me to have a good time. My son didn't even come to the airport to say goodbye. He was hanging out with his friends. He would see me when I got back, he said. I cried on the airplane while devouring several little bottles of vodka. The flight attendant refused to make eye contact with me as she swiped my credit card and handed over the bottles. As we flew over the Atlantic, it occurred to me that I had never really wanted to go to Europe in the first place. It was more that I wanted to be European. I wanted to be thin and rich and cultured while stuffing croissants in my face.

Once in Paris, I took a taxi to my hotel and lay on the bed and cried. I wanted water, but didn't know if the stuff out of the tap was good to drink. I missed the ubiquity of American hotel rooms. I worried that my sheets were dirty and I didn't like the way that the bed creaked when I lay down. I called my husband. He said, "Do you know how much this call is costing me?" I managed to leave the hotel in the evening to get a sandwich, one with crusty French bread and thinly sliced meat, and a bottle of sparking water that didn't taste at all the way I had expected it to.

3. Eat Smaller Portions

I had imagined myself strolling through churches and museums, sitting down to eat small, yet luxurious meals, and having my excess weight melt off me in a way it never had in the United States. I was a regular at the gym, Zumba, barbell strength, and spin classes and I still had these pockets of fat that I carried around with me. I had expected the new breasts to make me look smaller, but instead they made my whole body look busty and inappropriate, and I felt the need to cover up with a variety of sweaters that further obscured my shape.

Inexplicably, several days into the trip my feet started hurting. I hadn't brought my exercise shoes and only packed a pair of what I considered "smart" looking flats and a pair of heels for if I happened to come across a special occasion. I hadn't worn the flats much before leaving and that had perhaps been my mistake. I wandered into a store while in Brussels, hoping to find a new pair of shoes, and discovered that shoe sizes in Europe were totally different than sizes in America, and this extra hurdle was enough to dissuade me from my purchase, and I left the store and bought a waffle with whipped cream, strawberries, and chocolate syrup to soothe my feelings, and spent the rest of the night holed up in my hotel room with a stomachache.

Because of my aching feet, I only visited those tourist attractions that were described as "requisite" and even then I skipped some of those. There are a large multitude of beautiful churches in Europe, and when I walked into the first one in France, I was awed by the grandiosity of it. By the time I got to Italy, I had become used to the giant structures and preferred instead to find a nice restaurant and kill several hours by eating and drinking an extensive meal. Before going to Europe, I had fully intended to frequent only those little out-of-the-way spots known only to locals, but upon my arrival I realized that it was nearly impossible to find such eateries and settled for those heavily-advertised establishments along touristy streets where the servers spoke perfect English and understood American needs such as having large amounts of water and other beverages served throughout the meal. It occurred to me that perhaps all this talk about European thinness was based totally off water weight as I was constantly thirsty and no number of plastic water bottles was able to quench this thirst.

I knew that Europeans dined late and I imagined myself spending entire days strolling through museums and then settling down to a nice meal late in the evening. Finding myself incapable of strolling for hours at a time, I often went in search of restaurants around 5 PM, which was earlier than I ate in the U.S., and I was nearly always one of the only people eating at that time, except older American couples who also fell for the same tourist-trap restaurants that I did. I always felt better after housing a full meal and several glasses of wine though and would stumble back to my hotel room where I would take several Xanax and fall into a black sort of sleep where my body felt as though it wasn't in Europe or really anywhere at all.

I was surprised when my pants seemed to be getting tighter, my belly drooping over the waist. On one terrifying day, I'd had to wash my clothes in a laundromat in Germany and I told myself that it was the dryer that had caused my pants to shrink, and surely they would stretch out in no time. I didn't want to bother going into shops and trying to acquire new things to wear because it would just turn into the shoe debacle all over again, so I spent a great deal of time pants-less in my hotel room and had several housekeepers walk in on me that way, stuffing Toblerone into my face while wearing only underwear.

4. Don't Say Things You Don't Mean

I started to hate foreign languages. I still considered them foreign though they belonged to the places I went. I measured their foreignness from myself, the "I" at the center of it all.

The worst was Dutch. The words contorted their expressions. I had always thought that faces looked the same everywhere. I hadn't known that words could inherently change bone structure. Half of their alphabet sounded like a clearing of the throat, a perpetual bronchitis. It left them looking sour even when they did not speak. This is not to say that the Dutch were unkind. Everyone was kind to my wide American face. Later I learned that smiling was symptomatic of the United States. A false impression of perpetual happiness.

I started to resent all the people speaking languages I could not understand. Familiar characters appeared on the television, but their voices had been warped into something unrecognizable. "That's not what they sound like," I told my hotel room, which of course was foreign in its own way.

I found myself clinging to traveling groups of Americans. I hung out in hostel bars though I had an itinerary of nice hotel rooms booked. There were other single people traveling through hostels, people who wanted to go out and experience the nightlife. They told me that it was good that I was following my dreams at my age. Europe was not just for the young.

One night in Florence, after partaking in another decadent meal, I was walking past a bar on the way back to my hotel room when I became certain that my son was standing outside, smoking a cigarette. I knew that it couldn't be my son. The hair was all wrong and I never would have let him dress that way, but there was something about the stance, the way that he slouched over in avoidance of my gaze.

I followed him into the bar where I perched on a stool several feet away from the table where he sat with friends. Their loud American words punctured the music. I used to find it offensive the way everyone said Americans were loud, and used "loud" as an insult, as a synonym of classlessness. It was true, Americans were loud; I could hear every word of their conversation, I could see everything they were saying in their large gestures, and I loved it. If I closed my eyes, it was like momentarily being home.

I went over to their table. "Are you American?" I said. "Oh, thank god." I sat down without them asking me to. I bought the table a round of drinks. I was already quite drunk from dinner, but I was so happy to sit amongst this group and all of their Americanness that I was gulping beer down.

They were studying abroad, they said. They had been in Florence for two months. They were going to go home soon. One of the girls kept touching one of the guys' arm, not the one that looked like my son. The one that looked like my son was too little to draw attention. This other boy was the alpha male. I knew from the way the girl moved that she wanted him to love her, or at least wanted him to want to sleep with her, and that he didn't want to. He was resisting her motions, and I knew this resistance well. I wanted to give her guidance as an older woman. I knew what it was like not to be appreciated the way one ought to be appreciated.

"Do you want a Xanax?" I said to her. She made an American face of confusion and then an American face of "You're crazy." She told me, "No, thank you." She didn't like to take pills. I told them about how my husband had bought me breast implants and a trip to Europe. They all looked at my chest including the boy who was my son. I could tell from their tone that they pitied me. I didn't mind. I pitied myself.

The girl suggested that maybe my husband was cheating on me. I wanted to tell her that it was not polite to just say those sorts of things; she barely knew me. Instead, I vomited back into my beer glass. "Oh, no," I said. "Now I need another drink."

After my episode of vomiting, they wanted to leave the bar and move to a different location. No one invited me to come along, but I followed them down the cobbled streets. Florence wasn't beautiful the way I expected. Florence was full of fat tourists that looked like me except all of them were there as couples. No one travels to Italy alone. I grabbed my son's arm as we walked. "You look just like my son," I said. "Thank you," the boy replied though it wasn't a compliment. So like my son to not know what to say.

I only made it through part of a drink at the second bar before further sickening myself and spewing half-digested noodles across the floor. "You have to go home," the girl told me. I gave her an American look that said I hated her. I turned to my son and said, "Will you walk me home?" I didn't mean home, of course. Home was across an ocean. What I had meant to ask was "Will you walk me to my hotel?" He knew what I meant anyway. I could tell from his face that he didn't want to walk me to my hotel. I latched my arm around his shoulder. "Take me home," I said.

I was struggling to walk. My legs hurt and the boy was too small to support the weight of my body. "Maybe you can take a cab," he suggested. I wouldn't let go of his body. I knew that if I let go, he would leave. "Come upstairs with me," I said. My breath smelled like the insides of a stomach. "I will show you my breasts," I said in response to his hesitancy.

In my hotel room, we chugged down naturally carbonated water and I ate chocolate wishing it were bread. My son slipped his hand underneath my sweater. I was embarrassed by my stomach, all of those sandwiches and pizzas and gelatos. "Do they feel nice?" I asked him. I pulled his body close to mine and he let me. This was when I knew he wasn't really my son. My real son would never have let me touch him like that.

He got nervous when I tried to take his boxers off and told me he had to get back to his host-parent's house before the buses stopped running. I don't know what time it was when he left. I missed my train the next day. I went back to the bar where I had seen him the night before, but he wasn't there. I tried washing my shirt in the sink to get the vomit out and ended up throwing it in the garbage.

5. Fear of Nudity

I had sex with only one man while in Europe. I say only, but one is enough or too much depending on how I feel about my husband or my body or myself. He wasn't European. No Europeans talked to me unless they were serving me something and I was giving them money for those services.

He was Australian and he told me that my trip was a very Australian thing to do. I was flattered that someone thought I was part of a culture beyond my own, even if my knowledge of Australia consisted entirely of criminals and venomous animals. We met in the hotel lobby bar. I had assumed at the time we met that he was staying in the same hotel as me and learned later that he was actually just looking for a place to stay. I should've known there was a reason he carried his backpack around with him for the entire evening. He was the type of Australian animal that fed on lonely older women in nice hotels. He asked if I would buy him a drink. I was charmed by his forwardness. I told him I would do him one better and would buy him dinner. I was in Spain at this time, and we were the only ones in the restaurant. I told the servers to just keep the food coming. He was the first person I'd met in my travels who could put food back at the same rate that I could. We went out afterwards to a bar where we were the only white people there. I told myself that I was less white because I was American. We danced for hours and then went back to my hotel room where he leaned me over the bed in a position that I hadn't folded myself into for years. Afterwards he held me while I imagined all of our future travels together. I thought about calling my husband

and telling him that I had found someone new to love, someone who actually wanted to travel with me.

The next morning he went out for breakfast and never came back. What a clichéd move, I would've told him if I ever saw him again. I went to an Internet café and searched for his name, but there was no evidence that he had ever existed. I skipped breakfast that morning and made up for it by eating an entire pizza for lunch. I didn't care that I was in the wrong country for pizza. Pizza was good everywhere except Austria where they skimped on the sauce and dipped the slices in ketchup.

The entire trip existed as a countdown. The number of hours in a station until the next train. The number of days until I could return home. The minutes until I could eat a meal. How to get from one place to the next place.

My husband met me when I got off my return flight. I wanted him to see the visceral changes that had occurred inside of me while I was gone, the bad American habits I had broken, to call me European. Instead he said, "You ate a lot while in Europe," and laughed and made me get my own bag off the baggage claim. He took me to a French restaurant where I explained all the food to him even though I didn't really know anything. I told him about my trip even though he didn't really listen. "Ah, yes," I said when they brought out the escargot. "Those are snails."

Eventually They All Get Sick

The problem with mothers is eventually they all get sick.

It was expected that Drew would continue with school while his mother was sick. Drew, after all, was quite healthy. Drew liked to play pick-up basketball after school. Strawberry Pop-Tarts were his favorite food, though when his mother was well she encouraged him to eat more vegetables.

His mother's illness was both the slow-festering kind and the quick-killing kind. It was slow and festering in that she had been sick for several months and had become entirely bedridden and dependent on 24-hour care. It was quick killing in that in the days and weeks before her illness, she was perfectly healthy aside from a small cold and a couple bouts of mild diarrhea. The day she found out she was ill the doctors told her with no uncertainty that she was going to die and she was going to die soon.

Drew wasn't at the appointment. He was sitting in math class where he was drawing a series of cartoon figures in his notebook. When his mother found out she was going to die, she was alone aside from the doctors and the doctors in this circumstance could not be regarded as people.

Drew's mother didn't tell him she was going to die. Drew's mother also didn't tell him when his father left. Drew's mother said things like, "Eat more broccoli, it's healthy for you," and "Go do your homework." She never said things like, "I am rapidly dying."

It took Drew awhile to notice that the spots inside the toilet were dried vomit and that his mother's thick black hair was slowly receding and then, all at once, entirely gone. When he noticed he said, "I will eat one more bite of broccoli," and "I am doing my homework," even though he didn't actually eat more broccoli and had forgotten to write down his homework assignments.

Finally his mother said, "I'm going to the hospital," the same way that she said "I'm going to the grocery store," and Drew said, "Okay," and she had a taxi cab come and pick her up because she didn't want to pay for parking and Drew didn't have his driver's license yet.

He took the bus to the hospital after school and sat by his mother's hospital bed, which at first seemed like an immensely noble act, an act so sincere that he couldn't even tell his friends about it, but quickly became boring. Drew and his mother had little to talk about and spent most of their time watching daytime television. Drew's mother looked riveted, but only because she was too sick to move her eyes.

While his mother watched television Drew wandered the hospital trying to find a vending machine so that he could buy strawberry Pop-Tarts. The thing about the hospital is that no one ever feels like they belong there, even when they do, even when they are sick and dying. Drew was not sick and dying. Drew was a healthy teenage boy who was made uncomfortable by the stares of people walking by and thus when he found a white lab coat hung on a hook in the hallway he slipped it on. Because Drew was such a healthy boy, because Drew was tall and broad shouldered, the white lab coat fit him perfectly.

In the white lab coat he was nearly invisible as he wandered the halls. Hospitals are haunted by all sorts of things, doctors being the most prominent of all. It was the first time that Drew didn't feel scrutinized for the placement of his body. No one asked if he was supposed to be there or suggested that he would be better off going somewhere else.

He walked downstairs to the pediatric unit and stared at the room of babies through the glass. Drew didn't think babies were cute. Drew had been taught in school that babies were something to be afraid of. "Babies ruin your life," his health teacher had said. He peered into the room of little life-ruiners, their wrinkled little faces and pastel-colored hats. Drew and the life-ruiners had something in common in that all of them had mothers in the hospital as well. The difference was that the life-ruiners were responsible for their mothers' hospitalization, while Drew was a mere bystander in his mother's ravaging illness.

He walked down another flight of stairs and through a series of doors until he found the X-ray room. No one was being X-rayed, but he knew what it was from the time that he broke his arm on the playground when he was eight years old. He had been climbing on things that he wasn't supposed to be climbing on. He was up too high.

His mother told him to come down and he didn't listen. He never listened. Part of being a child was not listening to parents when they gave warnings about things. When he fell his mother said, "I told you that would happen," and then she sighed and found someone with a cellphone because they were still too expensive for her to buy and sat and held the hand attached to his healthy arm all the way to the E.R. and then sat with him three hours more while they waited for a doctor to see him.

"This will teach you not to climb on things," she said and then purchased him a soda out of the vending machine to make him feel better.

Drew climbed on top of the X-ray table. He wanted to see the insides of his body. The problem with pretending to be a doctor was that he had no one to examine him because he was supposed to be doing the examination. There were some X-rays hanging from the examination lights and he turned them on and told the empty room his analysis. "Everything is broken," he said. "You need new arms, new legs, and a new brain." He then did an imitation of the patient crying out, "No, doctor, tell me something good."

When the sun went down he returned and sat with his mother. He ate most of the food from her dinner tray because she said she wasn't hungry. Drew couldn't remember a time that his mother hadn't been hungry before, but he was so grateful to be eating a bread roll that he didn't say anything, worried that she would change her mind and take the roll away.

He took the last bus home in the evening. His mother had washed all of the dishes and stocked the kitchen with food before she left, but she had forgotten to teach Drew how to cook and thus everything in the kitchen had begun to rot. Drew didn't know that everything was rotting. Drew did not know what rot looked like. His mother had always used everything in their kitchen before it went bad, eventually mixing everything together and calling it "stir-fry."

"Why can't we just go out?" Drew said nightly.

"Because I made this meal for you," his mother replied.

Drew did not know what it meant to make a meal because he had never made one before. He got a strange urge for stir-fry and was disappointed when he walked into the kitchen and found all of the groceries neatly put away in their place and not stir-fried at all.

The first few mornings when his mother was in the hospital Drew dutifully walked down the street and waited for the yellow school bus to come and bring him to school. Finally it occurred to him that without his mother there was no one to tell him to go to school. Drew understood that in the greater scheme of things there were many reasons to go to school, but on a day-to-day basis his main motivation for attending his classes was his deep fear of his mother's wrath. His mother had become too ill to harbor any wrath and thus Drew stopped attending school. Instead of attending school Drew put on his white lab coat and a pair of blue scrubs he had stolen out of a supply closet. Instead of attending school Drew became a doctor.

At first Drew commuted from his house to the hospital, gathering quarters in his pocket for the ride. That was before he was given a swipe card with his picture on it that gave him access to the doctor's lounge which had several cots for resting, a locker where he could store his extra clothes, and a vending machine that contained strawberry Pop-Tarts. The nurses chided him for losing his original swipe card and told him not to do it again. "Doctors," they said and chuckled. Drew didn't tell them that he never had an original swipe card or that he was actually supposed to be in high school and not the hospital. He liked his doctor I.D. card much better than his high school I.D. card. His high school I.D. card didn't get him anything except a discount at the movies.

It took Drew awhile to settle on a specialization. He wandered from the sleep lab to the cardiac unit and finally settled on the Emergency Room. There was something comforting about being around people in a panicked state. Their panic made Drew's own emotional state feel very calm in comparison. While these people bled and cried, Drew had a doctor's I.D. card and a white lab coat. He wasn't crying or bleeding at all. He was fine.

According to the other doctors on the E.R. floor, Drew was a resident and not a real doctor. This was fine with Drew because it meant that he didn't have to know everything the way that real doctors did and they still let him do stuff like stitch up wounds and set broken bones. He liked working with children the best. The children in the E.R. were acquiescent to his instruction and never questioned his capability as a doctor. Whereas adults, the whiners, never stopped asking questions.

"How many times a day do I take this pill?"

"Where did you go to medical school?"

"Are you sure it isn't broken?"

"You look too young to be a doctor."

After work, Drew and some of the other residents went out for drinks. He wasn't carded at the bar because he was with a whole group of doctors-in-training and surely a doctor must be over the age of 21. Drew got drunk for the first time. He spent a long time discussing with the other residents their favorite video games. They told him he was a cool dude and then he excused himself to go throw up. It was the best night he ever had. The residents made his high school friends seem so lame.

The next day there was a bus accident and the Emergency Room was swamped with patients with ruptured organs and broken bones. Some people wheeled in from ambulances were dead upon arrival. Drew had never seen a dead person before. The dead people looked almost like living people, except there was something eerie about the stillness of their chests. The area surrounding the dead was calm. No one panicked over a person no longer breathing.

Drew assisted a doctor in organ removal. He wasn't sure which organ it was. It turns out that almost all the organs look the same. The doctor complimented Drew on his ability to maintain a cool composure in a crisis.

"We need more people like you," the doctor said. Drew had never felt so proud.

When the emergency was under control, Drew went to the doctor's lounge to take a breather and eat some strawberry Pop-Tarts. The filling in the Pop-Tarts looked nothing like actual blood, something Drew had seen a lot of that day, but looked enough like fake blood that he felt mildly sick while he was eating and threw the second Pop-Tart in the trashcan, something that he had never done before.

Drew had lost weight since becoming a doctor without school lunch and his mother's dinners to sustain him.

It had been awhile since he had seen his mother. The last time he was in her room she was struggling to breathe and they put her on oxygen. The oxygen mask covered her face enough that she no longer looked like his mother.

"I don't want to remember her that way," he had overheard one of the Emergency Room patients say about their elderly mother who had fallen and broken a hip and Drew borrowed the rhetoric for his own mother. He didn't want to remember her that way.

He treated an old man with pneumonia.

He treated a child with a broken leg. He was getting good at masking casts.

He sent a girl who had swallowed too many pills to the psychiatric ward. She screamed at him that he was doing the wrong thing and he said to her, "Have you been to medical school?"

He watched a woman push a baby out of her womb.

He went to the Emergency Room holiday party and drank too much and sang karaoke.

He stitched a cut from cooking.

He helped a woman file claims with the police after her boyfriend beat her.

In the doctor's lounge Drew found a red onion. He used a scalpel to cut it open. It made his eyes run. He tried one of the pieces. It burnt his tongue. In the Emergency Room a drug addict handed him a tomato and asked for a prescription in return. One of the residents gave him a leftover container of rice.

"You look hungry, man," the resident said.

From the lost-and-found Drew grabbed a hotplate. He stole a bottle of soy sauce from the cafeteria, some broccoli from the salad bar. He kneeled down over the hot plate, careful not to spill on his white doctor's coat. He mixed together the chopped onion, tomato, broccoli, and rice. He poured soy sauce over the mixture.

He sat in one of the waiting room chairs and ate his meal. It was too salty, the vegetables undercooked. Drew ate it anyway. He needed the sustenance. As he ate he watched an old man wheeled in, clutching his heart. A gigantically pregnant woman clutching her crotch. A boy with seemingly nothing wrong at all except for the tears streaming down his face. The broccoli slid down Drew's throat, rooting itself inside of him. His stomach started to rumble and because Drew didn't have a doctoral degree, he could only guess at what that meant.

Acknowledgements

I owe a ton of gratitude to the following people and organizations that helped me write this book: Split Lip Press, Amanda Miska, Jayme Cawthern, Michael Martone, Chad Simpson, Joel Brouwer, Wendy Rawlings, Kellie Wells, Robin Metz, Monica Berlin, Nick Regiacorte, Shannon Hannigan, John Colburn, Tabitha Blankenbiller, Leesa Cross-Smith, the Knox College Public Relations Office, the University of Alabama English Graduate Office, Egan's Bar, Writer Twitter, and a special thank you to my dad and Brian Oliu.

Thank you also to the journals where some of these stories were previously published: Will Work 4 Food at *Word Riot*, Love Like Cheeto Residue That Never Comes Off The Fingers at *Pank*, Fever at *Literary Orphans*, Things Inside Of Us at *The Collagist*, Conjoined at *Psychopomp*, Carnival Surprise at *Vending Machine Press*, Mr. Skull (formerly Mr. Skull and the Russian) at *Pithead Chapel*, The Yellow Facemask at *Cleaver Magazine*, 5 Bad American Habits I Broke While Traveling Through Europe at *Blacktop Passage*, Eventually They All Get Sick at *Rappahannock Review* and Charlize with Many Hands at *Elmhurst Literary Magazine*.

NOW AVAILABLE FROM

General Motors
by Ryan Eckes

Fruit Mansion
by Sam Herschel Wein

Felt in the Jaw
stories by Kristen N. Arnett

Gather Us Up and Bring Us Home
stories by Shasta Grant

I Once Met You But You Were Dead
by SJ Sindu

For more info about the press and our titles, visit our website:
www.splitlippress.com

Find us on Facebook:
facebook.com/splitlippress

Follow us on Twitter:
@splitlippress

Made in the USA
Middletown, DE
26 March 2019